REAL PRESENCE

Other Crossway Books by Leanne Payne

The Broken Image
Crisis in Masculinity
Healing of the Homosexual

REAL PRESENCE

The Christian Worldview of
C. S. Lewis as Incarnational Reality

Leanne Payne

CROSSWAY BOOKS • WESTCHESTER, ILLINOIS
A DIVISION OF GOOD NEWS PUBLISHERS

To my mother, Forrest Williamson Mabrey,
who thoroughly understood
incarnational reality—
and lived it

CONTENTS

FOREWORD

It is a privilege for me to write an introduction to the new edition of Leanne Payne's book, *Real Presence*. Perhaps the best place to begin is to say why I, a Jesuit priest, happen to enjoy this privilege.

I can remember my first meeting with Leanne. It took place about five years ago at a Christmas party in Milwaukee at the home of some mutual friends. I had never met her, nor heard of her. She autographed a copy of *Real Presence* and gave it to me as a Christmas gift. I have to confess that I put it aside. I didn't read it until a few months later when I needed something to read on a plane and had nothing else at hand. So I took it with me. It turned out to be a memorable experience. I felt that she was saying in a deeper and fuller way things which I had thought of for so many years, but never expressed as well. In things where I thought myself a "pro," I found I was still an apprentice.

So impressed was I with her book that I asked if she would come to teach in a program in "Christian Spirituality" at Creighton University where I teach. Happily she found time in her busy schedule to accept. From these contacts, then, over the past few years our friendship has deepened.

This new edition carries a new title. The title of the

first was: *Real Presence: The Holy Spirit in the Works of C. S. Lewis.* Both the new and old title are apt titles for the book. The first title emphasized the Holy Spirit as the originating source of the transformation that takes place in us, which is called "incarnational reality." The new title lays stress on the fact that this theme constitutes not simply an aspect of Lewis's thought. It is at the very center of his view of the whole of reality. As St. Paul describes it, the whole of reality is changed by being taken up into Christ. "For anyone who is in Christ, there is a new creation, the old creation is gone, and the new one is here" (2 Cor. 5:14). That is what incarnational reality means. It forms the optic through which Lewis views the whole.

The aptness of this expression "incarnational reality" to describe Lewis's worldview comes from the fact that in Lewis the natural desire for truth that belongs to every human being took on the characteristic of an uncanny instinct. This came from a special gift of the Holy Spirit. It was a kind of "homing" instinct for reality that had been reoriented by Christ's redemption. This instinct was in his deep-heart. It guided his thoughts, his choice of words, the images that make up his imaginative stories.

Lewis, then, had a spiritual instinct for what we could call the "constellation of the real": Christ-sacrament-symbol-Spirit-Church-Scripture-mind-heart-imagination. In a letter to me, when I asked Leanne what I should do in this foreword, she wrote: "That is exactly what I tried to do: constellate the precious reality that is ours, but that most modern Christians seem so far from grasping. What needs to be done in this foreword, it seems to me, is to say that Lewis is such a gift to us because he did indeed put all this together."

I do not want to turn this foreword into an article on

Lewis. But I want to try to say as briefly as I can how "he did put all this together." I shall do this in a three-stage process: first, by pointing out the importance of the word "transposition" for Lewis; secondly, by showing how the metaphor of "weight" translates Lewis's notion of levels of transposition; finally, by referring to *The Screwtape Letters* to show how incarnational reality is not simply a neutral reality. Rather, it describes the presence of Christ and His mission in the world through the power of the Spirit. It lives, then, in constant counterpoint with the power of evil, which is by its nature anti-incarnational-presence.

First of all, then, "transposition" is the "power of the higher to come down and be incarnate in the lower." This is something that we are always doing, though we are not conscious of it. For example, we put thoughts (the higher) into writing on a sheet of paper (the lower); Beethoven, Mozart, Michelangelo put the higher (their inspiration) into notes on a score or into paint on a wall. These are all instances of transposition.

Theologically, the term is used to describe the "descents" of God into His creation: for example, how at creation God breathes His Spirit into the clay, and man takes on the likeness of God. The Incarnation is described as the transposition of the Word who was with the Father from all eternity into our human condition: "The Word was made flesh." Christ transposes His mission into His apostles: " 'As the Father sent me, so am I sending you.' After saying this he breathed on them and said: 'Receive the Holy Spirit . . .' " (John 20:21, 22). The Holy Spirit is transposed into our hearts: "The love of God has been poured into our hearts through the Holy Spirit who has been given to us" (Rom. 5:5).

In the second place, the metaphor that Lewis uses to describe this transposition of the higher into the lower is weight. The title that he gave to a sermon preached at St. Mary the Virgin, Oxford, in 1941 was "The Weight of Glory." It was his way of describing the meaning and dignity of the human person. Through transposition of God's creative Spirit, we become the image and likeness of God; and through the gift of the re-creating Spirit at baptism, we take on the image of Christ.

Weight is another term for value, or the heaviness, the worth of the real, especially incarnational reality. The relative weight or worth of the human person on the level of nature takes on the absolute worth of Christ through the transposition of His Spirit. Incarnational reality then, as I mentioned above, is described by St. Paul as a New Creation.

This leads me, then, to the third aspect of incarnational reality as portrayed in *The Screwtape Letters*. In this connection, it also serves to highlight the importance of Lewis's thought for today, and in particular for a new edition of Leanne Payne's book.

The very structure of incarnational reality is the paschal mystery, the cross and the resurrection. It is the victory over sin, death, and the Prince of Darkness. This victory, however, while decisive for the whole of the world, has to be appropriated by each individual with the help of God's grace. But the powers of evil are still present. We must, as St. Paul said, "Put on God's armor so as to be able to resist the devil's tactics" (Eph. 6:11).

There are two major problems: first, to recognize evil as evil, and to combat it; but even more difficult, the problem of recognizing evil where it simulates what is good. "It is not every spirit, my dear people, that you can trust; test them, to see if they come from God, there are many false prophets, now, in the world" (1 John 4:1). "If Satan himself goes disguised as an angel of light, there is no need to be surprised when his servants, too, disguise themselves as the servants of righteousness" (2 Cor. 11:14).

The Screwtape Letters are the description of the drama that takes place in the life of a person who moves from one level of incarnational reality to another by eluding the look-alikes and choosing the truly real. The strategy of the Devil is always the same: to empty incarnational reality of its inner weight; then to simulate the goodness associated with incarnational reality, even though the reality is not there. Once a person chooses that simulation, even perhaps basing his life on it, he has been hooked by emptiness that has been given the look of fullness. A person has based his life on something that never existed.

Certain chapters in Leanne Payne's book—"The Whole Intellect," "The Whole Imagination I: Surprised by Joy," The Whole Imagination II: The Two Minds"— are especially important to see how this process of emptying and simulation take place. The whole intellect is the power of the understanding through the light of faith to be receptive to the whole of truth. The power of evil attempts to filter out aspects of the truth, leaving a person with only parts of it. Then the simulation takes place in giving the part the appearance of the whole.

The whole imagination is the way the imagination is open to those images into which are transposed the "more" of God's revealed truth. When these images touch the deep-heart, they are accompanied by a profound joy. The whole imagination comes from the way that the deep-heart is influenced by the Holy Spirit in those aspects of our thinking and willing which are preconceptual—that is, unconscious mind.

When the heart, the mind, the imagination, the unconscious lose that weightedness that comes from the contact with incarnational reality through the spirit, then the emptied person becomes separated from the very roots of incarnational reality. He becomes the prey of any and every simulation of reality. In the words of St. Paul, he will be "tossed one way and another and carried along by every wind of doctrine, at the mercy of tricks that men play and their cleverness in practicing deceit" (Eph. 4:14). On the other hand, incarnational reality is a progressive taking on of the reality of Christ: "If we live by the truth and in love, we shall grow in all ways into Christ." We will have within ourselves the weight of glory, the presence of Christ through His Spirit.

I welcome, then, the new edition of Leanne Payne's book. May it have the wide circulation it deserves. For, after all, there are only two choices open to us: incarnational reality, or emptiness.

John R. Sheets, S.J.
Creighton University

PREFACE

How tremendous is this power available to us
who believe in God. That power is the
same divine energy which was
demonstrated in Christ when He raised Him
from the dead.
Ephesians 1:19, 20 (Phillips)

This book is written primarily for all who have loved
and benefited from the writings of C. S. Lewis, but it
is also for those who would like to step for the first
time into Lewis's unique world of understanding.
One can only marvel at the Holy Spirit's use of Lewis's
talents—not only in the life of the individual believer,
but in the ongoing renewal that the Church is experiencing today. The effectiveness of his writings is such
that it reaches an amazingly diverse audience of all
ages, levels, and backgrounds. Books by Lewis are
found in the homes of evangelicals, on the book-
shelves of Anglican rectories, Roman convents, university libraries, and in renewal communities. One
hears Lewis quoted on a myriad of subjects in every
place from television talk-shows to college lectures.
One Episcopalian bishop was overheard to remark: "It
is almost embarrassing the way I find myself quoting

Lewis so often, but the plain fact is, he simply says everything better than anyone else." Even young children quote Aslan and the talking beasts of Narnia, hanging their sayings on nursery walls. So it is that in the hearts and minds of a great many people indeed the writings of Lewis have found a permanent home.

The reason why this should be is easily understood: Lewis points a scholarly, imaginative, and thoroughly devout finger at the Real, firmly believing that It *is*. Then, great logician that he is, he methodically unmasks all the precious idols that we have substituted for reality. The reality of God, present in and through His creation, is what I shall call *incarnational reality*. Lewis puts us in touch with incarnational reality. His effectiveness lies in the fact that he touched this reality. Like the Galilean woman, he walked through the throng and touched Jesus. Like her, he found himself in the midst of the Real Presence. Like her, he was made whole as the divine energy issued forth and revitalized him in the deepest recesses of his being. This energy, this reality, fills his writings; it is, after all, the Presence of God—that Presence we all are either running from or searching for.

Most of us hunger for this reality. We do not know who we are until we find our own truest selves in God. It is the work of the Holy Spirit to call us up out of the hell of our false selves and into the glorious Presence of our Lord. And it is as we touch Him that His life, His Holy Spirit enters our being and we are indwelt by the living God. "The Christ that is formed in [the Christian]," Lewis wrote, "transforms every part of him: in it his spirit, soul and body will all be reborn."[1] The body is not to be understood as merely a "container" of the Holy Spirit, but as wed to the Spirit; it too is in the state of being "drawn up into the

Spirit." Man is indwelt by God, in every atom and molecule. It is Lewis's experience and understanding of incarnational reality that informs his vision of man's relationship to God, in which God redeems man from his fragmented and alienated condition. It is the aim of this book to help show how far-reaching and urgently needed that vision is.

There is no way I can adequately express my love and thanks to Dr. Clyde S. Kilby and Dr. Robert Siegel for the golden hours of talk about Lewis and his fellow Inklings. Without Dr. Kilby's interest in these writers and consequent founding of the Marion E. Wade Collection at Wheaton College, and without Dr. Siegel's invaluable critique of the manuscript, it is safe to say this book would never have seen the light of print. My heartiest thanks also go to the Rt. Rev. William C. Frey who not only read the manuscript carefully but gave the encouragement that only a bishop can give, to Prof. Helen Devette, who first "saw to it" that the manuscript got out of my hands and into the hands of an editor; to Luci Deck Shaw, Prof. Carol Kraft, Herman and Lillie Riffel, Dr. H. Wilbert Norton, Gayle Sampson, and Rhoda L. Hegberg for their prayerful encouragement. I also wish to thank Madeleine L'Engle for her gracious permission to quote her within the pages of this book, and to Mr. Walter Hooper for his generous permission to publish from the Lewis Letters in the Wade Collection.

1

INTRODUCTION:
INCARNATIONAL REALITY

*"When Christians say the Christ-life is in
them, they do not mean simply something
mental or moral. When they speak of being
'in Christ' or of Christ being 'in them,' this is
not simply a way of saying that they are
thinking about Christ or copying Him. They
mean that Christ is actually operating
through them; that the whole mass of
Christians are the physical organism through
which Christ acts—that we are His fingers and
muscles, the cells of His body."*
Mere Christianity.

It was nearly a decade ago that I first encountered the
world of C. S. Lewis. What began as a brief tour has
become a most refreshing and challenging adventure.

It began under the guidance of Dr. Clyde S. Kilby, a
man who has given most of his professional life to
making known the writings of Lewis. In Lewis Dr.
Kilby found "a mind sharp as a scalpel and as intent as
a surgeon upon the separation of the diseased from
the healthy." Dr. Kilby's "impression was of a man
who had won, inside and deep, a battle against pose,

evasion, expedience, and the ever-so-little lie and who wished with all his heart to honor truth in every idea passing through his mind."[1] I too was caught up by the power and the integrity of such a mind—one that could simply and with apparent ease cut away all substitutes for the real and point to the reality itself for all to see. The words "incarnational reality" kept recurring to me as I studied the writings of Lewis; for I saw his effectiveness to be rooted in a living and comprehensive understanding of the Holy Spirit's indwelling of the very being of the Christian.

For Lewis, to know God was to be invaded by His Spirit; as Christians we are both "in Christ" and "He in us." St. Paul's statement, ". . . not I but Christ that liveth in me,"[2] formed the center of Lewis's theology and philosophy. It was, in fact, the experience of the "living presence" of God that eventually brought Lewis from a form of philosophical idealism (belief in "Absolute Spirit") to a supernatural knowledge of a personal God—of a Real Presence, within and without. For himself and for many others, Lewis recovered the vision of an immanent God—a God who indwells His people—Who is yet sovereign over, and beyond, His creature. Knowing well that Christians had for the most part lost this understanding, and that the non-Christian of the twentieth century had not even an inkling of it, Lewis proclaimed in philosophical, theological, and imaginative terms that the creature is linked—and can be absolutely linked—to the Creator.

In Lewis I found a true Christian philosopher—one who was convinced that to know God was to be indwelt by Him. The creature is linked to the Creator by the Spirit of the risen Christ. This fact, fully comprehended and experienced, is the "whole of it," as Lewis would say. The Kingdom of God has come among us and into us. To accept this truth is both to understand, and to know experientially, the presence of the Holy Spirit. But, as Lewis points out, this is the one truth that man tends always to fall away from. Left to his natural inclinations, he evades its "awe-ful" reality, and invents for himself shallow and less demanding substitutes for his one redeeming link with God.

God by His Spirit may indwell man; Christians are therefore linked with the Absolute. With brilliant clarity, Lewis reveals that over this view of reality all the philosophies and ideologies of man stumble. Herein is Christianity different from all other religions. Unless one is literally filled by the Real Presence of the risen Christ, he cannot see the Kingdom of God. The infinite God is united with the dependent and the derived, with the feeble and mortal, by His Holy Spirit. This Holy Spirit, indwelling a man, is capable of reviving the whole personality. Every faculty of man is to be developed and used to the glory of God Who is saving man to the uttermost and Who will bring to perfection the work which He has begun.

Lewis has said much more about the Holy Spirit, and from a higher perspective—though his terminology of the Third Person, like that of the New Testament and the early Church Fathers, is marvelously implicit—than many who write explicitly about Him today. He speaks most often of the Father and the Son. Yet, just as in the person of Jesus Christ, God Himself became incarnate, so after Pentecost the risen Christ indwells the believer by the descent of the Holy Spirit. These descents illustrate what is for Lewis a key principle in the universe—what he calls "transposition." Transposition is the power of the higher to come down and be incarnate in the lower. For instance, reason thus becomes incarnate in the natural man: "that relatively supernatural element . . . given to every man at his creation—the rational element"[3] is transposed into a body. Likewise, the human spirit descends to become incarnate in the physical body, and human thought in the senses and passions: "We catch sight of a new key principle—the power of the Higher, just in so far as it is truly Higher, to come down, the power of the greater to include the less."[4] God has come down to us and we can know Him by His Spirit indwelling us. Further, all reality is "but a faint image of the Divine Incarnation itself."[5]

When one surfaces from a plunge into Lewis's world, he generally takes an unprecedented and swift flight upward into a universe that is not only greatly expanded but has been given back its supernatural reality. Its transcendent realm is no longer hidden. The fetters of unbelief snap and he soars the free heights with Lewis. As both philosopher and novelist, Lewis reveals the whole of reality to us that we might better apprehend the parts; he reveals the Creator to us that we might better understand creation. In his cosmic view of supernature and nature, we see that God reaches down to man; that man is, indeed, linked with God. The very concreteness of the realities we have all too often abstracted away (including the supernatural) returns. We have restored to us, not only the knowledge of the Holy Spirit, but of angels, demons, and all the hosts of heaven. And within our very own selves we find a root—"a root in the Absolute, which is the utter reality."[6]

2

GOD, SUPER-NATURE, AND NATURE

" 'Who do you speak to, Hrikki?' said
Ransom.
" 'To the eldil [angel].'
" 'Where?'
" 'Did you not see him?'
" 'I saw nothing.'
" 'There! There!' she cried suddenly. 'Ah!
He is gone. Did you not see him?'
" 'I saw no one.'
" 'Hyoi!' said the cub, 'the hman *cannot*
see the eldil!' "
Out of the Silent Planet.

God Who has no opposite is, according to Lewis,
the most concrete, the most individual, thing there is.
He is "basic Fact or Actuality, the source of all other
facthood."[1] While it is impossible that our an-
thropomorphic images of God can fully reflect His
Presence within, without, and all about us, our
abstractions of Him can be even more harmfully mis-
leading. After all, "What soul ever perished for believing God the Father really has a beard?"[2] On the other
hand, He Who is ultimate Reality often eludes us in

our abstractions about Him. We find ourselves in the same situation as Charles Williams's character, Damaris,[3] who compares the medieval ideas of the Platonic *Eidola*[4] with those of the Christian *Angeli*,[5] but who has no real care for eidola, nor belief in angels, since her interest is only an intellectual one. Like many in Christendom, she delves deep into ideas about concrete realities but at the same time holds them away from herself on an abstract level. Lewis would say that the attitude of Damaris is exactly why so much of our theology is ineffective today. Somewhere along the line, many of us in Christendom have played down direct knowledge of the supernatural, of the fact that God can reveal Himself to man by His presence. Sitting in the midst of great realities, studying them while lacking a positive intuition or experience of them, we hold them far away from ourselves. Surely our fear of naive anthropomorphism should never drive us to a degree of theological abstraction that becomes a substitute for receiving experientially Reality Himself.

> Never, here or anywhere else, let us think that while anthropomorphic images are a concession to our weakness, the abstractions are the literal truth. Both are equally concessions; each singly misleading, and the two together mutually corrective. Unless you sit to it very tightly, continually murmuring "Not thus, not thus, neither is this Thou," the abstraction is fatal. It will make the life of lives inanimate and the love of loves impersonal.[6]

There have been many appearances of God to man recorded in the Scriptures, but these were "mediated" (or in Lewis's terminology, "transposed") appearances. Several of these recorded visitations were to

Moses. In Exodus 33, the Lord, descending in a pillar of cloud, speaks to Moses "face to face, just as a man speaks to his friend." He promises Moses that His presence will go with him and, furthermore, that He will give him rest as he attempts to lead the disobedient and stiff-necked children of Israel through the wilderness. It is then that Moses makes a request of God: "Show me Thy glory." Apparently Moses was not content to see only God's "mediated" Presence and asked to see Him face to face in all His glory. Moses is told, "You cannot see My face, for no man can see Me and live."[7] If the one whom Moses faced had revealed His full glory, Moses' mortal body could not have borne it.[8] Yet the Lord told Moses to stand by Him upon a rock, "And it will come about, while My glory is passing by, that I will put you in the cleft of the rock and cover you with My hand until I have passed by. Then I will take My hand away and you shall see My back, but My face shall not be seen."[9] After seeing God's glory as it was reflected from His back, Moses' face shone so that the children of Israel were afraid to come near him. He had to wear a veil except when he went in to minister unto the Lord, because he had experienced such concentrated exposure to God's Presence.

Lewis knew well that sinful man cannot bear to see God's face in all its glory. Indeed, in *The Silver Chair*, the fourth book in his celebrated children's series, *The Chronicles of Narnia*, Lewis has a scene recalling God showing His back to Moses on Mt. Sinai. Aslan the Lion, who represents God in these stories, is sending two children back to England after their adventures in the magical kingdom of Narnia. Jill asks Aslan if he is coming back to earth with them. He doesn't answer her directly, but says that the children will then see only his back though he will be present with them. Aslan then turns to the children, Jill and Eustace, and breathes upon them and touches their foreheads with his tongue: "Then he . . . turned his golden back to England, and his lordly face towards his own lands."[10]

God is no more an abstraction to Lewis than He was to Moses. To both men He was ultimate reality and capable of manifesting Himself, even though in a "mediated" or "transposed" form. Moses learned that God's radiant substantiveness had to be mediated by a form which his mortal eyes could bear to look upon. Lewis also learned this lesson, and the history of JOY in his life weaves the incarnational pattern of God's revelations.

This embodiment of spiritual reality in material form is the principle of the Incarnation; or in other words, it is the principle of sacramental truth whereby God's Real Presence is made manifest in and through the material world. The Incarnation was and is, of course, the most amazing and complete example of a mediated (i.e., a sacramental) reality. Since Christ ascended in the flesh, ultimate reality is known by man in union with Him through the Person of the Holy Spirit. As Aslan breathed his spirit into Jill and Eustace so Christ has given us His Spirit, and His Presence therefore remains with us. Though Lord of all and over all, He is also God with us and in us. We may desire, like Moses or like John, to see Him in all His glory—not just in visions, dreams, and in our sanctified imaginations. We may desire to see His angels, cherubim, seraphim, and even all the hosts of heaven gathered in one great choir, as we may one day see them. But we do not see God directly. Yet, though our finiteness limits our perceptions of God and the supernatural, we have no reason to reduce them to abstractions.

In his fiction[11] Lewis advanced a fascinating theory to explain why we mortals do not ordinarily see angels and other supernatural beings: their substance moves at a radically different rate of speed than ordinary matter. Moving swifter than light, their bodies are not ordinarily sensible to us (as trees and houses are); their usual invisibility is however no reason to relegate their shining reality to the grey regions of the abstract and the insubstantial. On the contrary, Lewis suggests, angels are so real that rocks and walls and all which seems solid to us is to them transparent and cloudlike. (It is interesting to reflect on this in light of modern physics which has shown that all the objects of our world which we presume to be solid are actually not at all.) It is a small thing for them to pass through the most solid of matter. If one is versed in the Gospel narrative, his imagination will quickly fly to the story of Christ's post-resurrection appearances to His disciples; we might speculate that Christ's radiant solidity was such that by contrast the walls were cloud-like and insubstantial:

> If anything is clear from the records of Our Lord's appearances after His resurrection, it is that the risen body was very different from the body that died and that it lives under conditions quite unlike those of natural life. It is frequently not recognized by those who see it: and it is not related to space in the same way as our bodies. The sudden appearances and disappearances suggest the ghost of popular tradition: yet He emphatically insists that He is not merely a spirit and takes steps to demonstrate that the risen body can still perform animal operations, such as eating. What makes all this baffling to us is our assumption that to pass beyond what we call

Nature—beyond the three dimensions and the five highly specialized and limited senses—is immediately to be in a world of pure negative spirituality, a world where space of any sort and sense of any sort has no function. I know of no grounds for believing this. To explain even an atom Schrödinger wants seven dimensions: and give us new senses and we should find a new nature. There may be Natures piled upon Natures, each supernatural to the one beneath it.[12]

Heaven and all it contains, according to Lewis, is of such reality that the unredeemed (those who have chosen self and hell) can never be at home in it. In *The Great Divorce*, Lewis pictures those who refuse redemption as insubstantial and even ghostlike. These "ghosts" choose hell because they cannot stand the utter reality of heaven. Even the green blades of grass on the outskirts of Paradise are of such a sharp solidity that they pierce through the visitors' transparent feet. The unredeemed, in choosing self rather than God, hell rather than heaven, have chosen insubstantiality rather than radiant substance. They have refused incarnational reality, the infusion of the Spirit of God into their empty and insubstantial beings.

The above explains what theologians mean when they use the term *inessential* in regard to evil. God creates; evil can only destroy, and this fact is fleshed out in a great theme that runs through the works of Lewis.[13] Good creates; evil can only destroy. Even so, his view of good and evil never allows him to dismiss Satan and demonic beings as merely mythic representations of the evil in man; they are intelligent powers, active in the world today. Man is not the only fallen creature; other beings suffer alienation from God. Satan, the destroyer and hater of all creation, is a personality and his angels are a present evil force the

Christian must withstand. In the Garden of Eden story there is the lesson of not only a *self* alienated from God but also of a *tempter* alienated from God. Lewis understands both lessons correctly. Unlike most of his contemporaries (who are in this respect descendants of the poet Blake), Lewis divorces heaven and hell. His fiction portrays man capable of an evil indwelling presence as well as of a good. In *Perelandra*, the protagonist Ransom, possessed by God's Spirit, is in stark contrast to the antagonist Weston; demonically possessed, the latter becomes the Unman, the grotesque parody of humanity to which Satan would like to reduce all men.

As there is no ultimate dualism in Christianity, so there is none in Lewis. God has no true opposite; Satan, a created being, is the opposite not of God but of the archangel Michael.[14] Because the malevolence of Satan and the fallen angels cannot create but only destroy, they continually fall toward the nothingness they have chosen, toward what is ultimately insubstantial. Even so, they are spiritual realities and not mere abstractions; they have actual being and are capable of working harm. Invisible though they are to the mortal eye, they are concrete entities over which Christians must take authority.

It is interesting in view of Lewis's theory of why we mortals do not ordinarily see spiritual beings to learn what physicists have to say about the extent of man's sensory limitations. Our eyes cannot see cosmic, gamma, or X-rays, nor ultraviolet, infrared, radar, television, or shortwave radio waves—not to mention other known and unknown wave lengths of light. The visible radiations of light form only a very small band on the electromagnetic spectrum of light known to exist. The eyes of man can receive only those radiations of light that fall within the rainbow colors of the solar spectrum. It is humbling to realize how little of this world's light we are capable of seeing. *And we would see the Father of Lights!* Man's other sensory organs are just as limited. What we ordinarily speak of as "the supernatural" may consist of those parts of creation beyond our narrow sensory capacity.

"The paradox of physics today," says physicist Lincoln K. Barnett, "is that with every improvement in its mathematical apparatus the gulf between man the observer and the objective world of scientific description becomes more profound."[15] So it is that physicists and scientists, in their acceptance of Einstein's mathematical description of the cosmos, have had to go beyond the world of sense perception and ordinary experience. The objective world of utter reality "can be encompassed in its entire majesty only by a cosmic intellect," says Barnett. He further states that it is a question among physicists, having passed over "the thin line that divides physics from metaphysics,"[16] as to "whether scientific man is in touch with reality at all."[17]

Though the merely scientific and sensory man may fail to do so, the Christian affirms with Lewis that the Spirit-indwelt man can touch reality. But an experiential understanding of the Holy Spirit is necessary first. Man can know the Presence, and only through the Presence can he know the reality of God and His creation. Otherwise, He is lost among the flickering shadows of appearances, where even the solid earth before Him can seem to fade into the abstractions of mathematics.

We come to know ultimate reality, not by theological ideas about it, even though these are valid and necessary, but by *union* with it—by the establishing of

a personal relationship between God and man. It begins in a meeting with God such as Abraham had
when he was called out of Ur; it develops into a union
and communion with God such as Paul describes in
these words: "I am crucified with Christ: nevertheless
I live; yet not I, but Christ liveth in me."[18] In union
with Christ, the whole of man's being becomes hallowed. The body, therefore, is not to be despised, nor
is it to be perceived as merely a "container" of the
Holy Spirit. Such a notion smacks of a dualism that
perceives matter as evil and spirit as good. Rather, the
body too is in the state of being drawn up into God:

> [W]e are told in one of the creeds that the Incarnation
> worked "not by conversion of the Godhead into flesh,
> but by taking of the Manhood into God." And it seems to
> me that there is a real analogy between this and what I
> have called Transposition: that humanity, still remaining
> itself, is not merely counted as, but veritably drawn into,
> Deity.[19]

Man is indwelt, in every atom and molecule. We are
both in Christ and He in us. The Spirit may be seen as
filling or even enveloping the body. This leads Lewis
to speculate on the state of the resurrected body:

> At present we tend to think of the soul as somehow
> "inside" the body. But the glorified body of the resurrec-
> tion as I conceive it—the sensuous life raised from its
> death—will be inside the soul. As God is not in space but
> space is in God. . . .
>   I don't say the resurrection of this body will happen at
> once. It may well be that this part of us sleeps in death,
> and the intellectual soul is sent to Lenten lands where she
> fasts in naked spirituality—a ghostlike and imperfectly
> human condition. . . . Yet from that fast my hope is that

we shall return and re-assume the wealth we have laid down.

Then the new earth and sky, the same yet not the same as these, will rise in us as we have risen in Christ. And once again, after who knows what aeons of the silence and the dark, the birds will sing and the waters flow, and lights and shadows move across the hills, and the faces of our friends laugh upon us with amazed recognition.

Guesses, of course, only guesses. If they are not true, something better will be. For "we know that we shall be made like Him, for we shall see Him as He is."[20]

There is no simple merging of man and God in this Christian union. Rather each man's uniqueness is enhanced and even glorified in a transposition which redeems his fallen nature and has for its final aim to set his "whole body free."[21] Every created thing, animate and inanimate, awaits the splendour of this freeing,[22] this revealing of God's adopted sons, because "the universe itself is to be freed from the shackles of mortality and enter upon the liberty and the splendour of the children of God."[23] All of nature will acknowledge in praise and adoration its Creator:

There may be Natures piled upon Natures, each supernatural to the one beneath it, before we come to the abyss of pure spirit; and to be in that abyss, at the right hand of the Father, may not mean being absent from any of these Natures—may mean a yet more dynamic presence at all levels.[24]

In contrast to some modes of Eastern religion which seem to pursue a union that would annihilate all distinctions, the Christian union and communion can exist only between distinct, differentiated entities. We, the creatures, are in union with the Creator. He

Who is the Uncreated made the created precisely so that He might love and commune with beings distinct from Himself. Lewis points out that the pantheistic aim of merging with the All is therefore a reversal, a doubling back on the path which God has mapped out for man; its goal is a type of unity which God has rejected. It is a "mere unity" as opposed to a true union and communion between separate beings:

> Pantheism is a creed not so much false as hopelessly behind the times. Once, before creation, it would have been true to say that everything was God. But God created: He caused things to be other than Himself that, being distinct, they might learn to love Him, and achieve union instead of mere sameness.[25]

In a true *union* there must be a coupling of differentiated entities, or the word would lose all meaning. In it there is no thought of annihilation, no desire for a nameless merging; rather, each person is led into a unique individuality from which he is capable of giving and receiving love. After all, one must be distinct and individual to truly love another. In union with God, the Christian becomes a son of God, always distinct from God the Father. By virtue of his being indwelt he achieves an immortal and unique being "begotten" by the Spirit of God.

To experience this union is to apprehend the Presence of God within and without. The most concrete reality that can be known, it is often relegated to the abstract and the theoretical by those who attempt to know it only with the conscious, analytical mind. But our sole avenue to reality is, as Lewis says, through prayer, sacrament, repentance, and adoration;[26] that is, through the deep heart's way of *knowing*. Knowing

here is not a "direct 'knowledge about' *(savoir)*" God,
but a " 'knowledge-by-acquaintance' *(connaître)*," a
" 'tasting,' of Love Himself" that "the humblest of us,
in a state of Grace," can know.[27]

3

SACRAMENT:
AVENUE TO THE REAL

*"What nature is in herself evades us;
what seem to naive perception to be the most
evident things about her, turn out to be the
most phantasmal. It is something of the
same with our knowledge of spiritual reality.
What God is in Himself, how He is to be
conceived by philosophers, retreats continually
from our knowledge. The elaborate
world-pictures which accompany religion and
which look each so solid while they last, turn
out to be only shadows. It is religion itself—
prayer and sacrament and repentance and
adoration—which is here in the long run,
our sole avenue to the real."*
"Dogma and the Universe,"
God in the Dock.

C. S. Lewis knew and experienced Christianity in
its sacramental context. The sacraments of baptism
and Holy Communion were for him not mere symbols
of union, but means by which the Real Presence and
the very life of Christ are channeled to believing man.
Speaking of the mystery of Holy Communion he said,
"Here a hand from the hidden country touches not
only my soul but my body. Here the prig, the don, the
modern in me have no privilege over the savage or the

child. Here is big medicine and strong magic."[1] To appreciate Lewis's full view of the Person and work of the Holy Spirit it is necessary, therefore, to understand the sacramental view of reality.

St. Paul taught that Christians form a mystical unity with one another through their fellowship with, and incorporation into, Christ.[2] The first-century Christians appear to have understood this unity, this fellowship, this incorporation into Christ better than we do today, perhaps because they experienced more fully the work of the Holy Spirit in their lives. Though they had as yet formulated no clear-cut doctrines of the Holy Spirit, they simply and daily experienced His power. Their unity was by virtue of immersion into this One Spirit. The charismatic structure[3] of the church was taken for granted, and each believer was a vital part of this structure, exercising his own "charism" or "gift." Besides this, each heard and received the ministry of the apostles and the prophets, men powerfully gifted by the Holy Spirit. These men were seen as having been specially empowered by the risen Christ to proclaim and disclose[4] the Real Presence of God among His people. The rites of baptism and the Lord's Supper were understood as special means by which God's grace was revealed and received—by which His Spirit was mediated to man. The same Spirit Who provided the unity, Who indwelt and gifted the believer, also mediated forgiveness, new strength, and the Real Presence of Jesus through these mysteries.[5]

These early Christians believed their unity to be not only symbolized, but actualized, in Holy Communion or the Eucharist; they believed that we are one with God and our brother by the one Lord mediated through this sacramental mystery. Just as they *experi-*

enced the Holy Spirit working through the apostles and prophets, so they experienced the presence of Christ through the Lord's Supper. Having received the New Birth and the Holy Spirit, they found themselves in a relationship anything but static and fixed. Rather they saw themselves as vessels, open always to the Spirit and continually receiving from Him. Always, their eyes were on God, receiving from Him and blessing Him in return.

The sacramental view of reality affirms that Spirit can be and is encountered in and through material forms. God Who is Spirit became man! Spirit does not despise "matter"; the Uncreated does not despise the created. Christ, born of Mary, dwelt among us in human form, and by doing so "has forever hallowed the flesh."[6] The sacramental view of reality understands that Christ's Incarnation, though perhaps the most amazing expression of God's loving descent into His own "matter," did not end when He ascended to the Father. Christ *is* risen, and is not only at the right hand of God the Father, but is also, by virtue of what began at Pentecost, risen *in us.*

> There is no good trying to be more spiritual than God. God never meant man to be a purely spiritual creature. That is why He uses material things like bread and wine to put the new life into us. We may think this rather crude and unspiritual. God does not: He invented eating. He likes matter. He invented it.[7]

This view understands that the Real Presence of God is encountered in and through the Communion elements. As Lewis's character Ransom learns, while visiting an unfallen planet, the sacraments remind us of the ultimate unity of the material and spiritual realms:

Long since on Mars, and more strongly since he came to
Perelandra, Ransom had been perceiving that the triple
distinctions of truth from myth and both from fact was
purely terrestrial—was part and parcel of that unhappy
division between soul and body which resulted from the
Fall. . . . [T]he sacraments existed as a permanent reminder the division was neither wholesome nor final.
The Incarnation had been the beginning of its disappear-
ance.[8]

Though uniquely Christian in its fullness, this view
is rooted in Judaism. Very simply, *sacramental reality
has to do with the means by which the Presence of God is
mediated to fallen man:* and, as a principle, it was in
effect before Christ, the "personalized core of Christian reality,"[9] descended into the flesh. Moses, we
recall, descended from the mountain radiant with the
glory of God.

Before the Fall, of course, man experienced God's
Presence continually. In *Perelandra,* Lewis depicts the
life of an unfallen planet and an unfallen Eve (the
Green Lady). The Green Lady, basking in pure goodness and listening always to Maleldil (God), is not
even aware that she is "separate" from Him. Unlike
the Green Lady, however, our first parents fell, and
the first thing they did was to hide themselves from
the Presence.[10] They knew themselves to be separate.

This is what the Fall was and is—separation from
the Presence. Man fell from God-consciousness into
the hell of self, and of self-consciousness. The history
of fallen man can be summed up as a flight from the
radiant substantiveness—the reality of the Presence
and the Face of God. Even then, after the Fall, there
was provision made for men to meet with a "mediated
Presence." They brought their blood sacrifices to the

altar where they worshipped and met with God. We are told that Cain, after he murdered his brother, was driven out from this Presence.[11] Generations later, when God commissioned Moses, He promised him, "My Presence shall go with you."[12] After Pharaoh capitulated, and the Exodus began, "The Lord went before them, by day a pillar of cloud to guide them on their journey, by night a pillar of fire to give them light, so that they could travel night and day."[13] Here is the Presence of God mediated visibly through the cloud and the pillar of fire.

Throughout the Psalms we see King David "practicing the Presence" of God:

I have set the Lord continually before me:
  with him at my right hand I cannot be shaken.
  Therefore my heart exults
    and my spirit rejoices,
  my body too rests unafraid;
  for thou wilt not abandon me to Sheol
  nor suffer thy faithful servant to see the pit.
    Thou wilt show me the path of life;
    in thy presence is the fullness of joy,
    in thy right hand pleasures for evermore.[14]

Similarly, Isaiah and the prophets are seen crying out to a backslidden people who have despised the mediated Presence and the prophets through whom this Presence speaks. They are therefore told that God will cause them as a nation to tremble, and that their cities will be broken down before the Presence of this Lord. Ezekiel, foreseeing Armageddon and the end of times, cries out as the mouthpiece of God: "All the men that are upon the face of the earth shall shake at My Presence."[15] Later we see the prophet Jonah fleeing from this awesome Presence only to find that he cannot run far enough from a loving God bent on saving a pagan people.[16]

The Old Testament Tabernacle was an earthly sanctuary made by Moses after the pattern God gave him of "heavenly things." The Tabernacle had a Holy of Holies within which rested the Ark of the Covenant. This Ark, like the Tabernacle itself, was also made according to the "shadow" of heavenly things. Inside the Ark dwelt the Uncreated, the Divine Presence, so powerfully that only the High Priest could enter the inner sanctuary and live.[17] To understand the special Presence in the Tabernacle and in the Ark is to understand, at least partially, sacramental reality. Israel knew that Yahweh was in His heaven, but they also knew that He was with them in a unique, if barely approachable, way in the Holy of Holies. After Christ, we as the new Israel are to know the Presence of God indwelling us. Individually and corporately we are *the Body*, the "Ark" or the "Temple" of the Presence—an idea almost staggering if we could truly comprehend it. We are the indwelt—the fellowship of the Holy Spirit.

We are told in the book of Hebrews that Christ Who is the Head of this Body of believers has, as our High Priest, passed through the heavens into the heavenly tabernacle not made by human hands, and there He appears in the Holy of Holies continually interceding for us: "For Christ is not entered into the holy places made with hands, which are the figures of the true; but into heaven itself, now to appear in the presence of God for us."[18] Whereas the priests of old entered at intervals into the earthly figure of the heavenly (to meet the Presence there), Christ entered once and for all, by His own blood, into that Holy of Holies where dwells that Light and Glory which is the undiluted, "unmediated" Being of the Uncreated. Now that He is, by this sacrifice, High Priest, the Presence is continually made available to us. The life in that blood-sacrifice of Christ, made once for all, flowed out to us and continues to do so as He continually intercedes for us. This is why He gives us the special command: "Take eat, this is My Body" when the fellowship meets together. The life is in the Presence, and the Presence is to be continually made available to us in and through the sacraments.

On the other hand, it is, as Lewis writes to his friend, Arthur Greeves, "so fatally easy to confuse an aesthetic appreciation of the spiritual life with the life itself."[19] It is easy to know, in apparent detail, the doctrines of the life in Christ without ever experiencing the life itself. Oddly enough, we have made objects out of vital acts and experiences. One almost hesitates in the face of the vitality of New Testament accounts of baptism to label this event by the word "sacrament." Perhaps we hesitate because the word's connotation is that of a "thing" or a doctrine rather than of an experience of the Holy Spirit full of mystery and awe. In the biblical accounts[20] we see the great mystery of God deigning to indwell man occurring in broad daylight. An ordinary man on an ordinary day is suddenly confronted with the Good News; he submits to the rites commanded by Christ and finds his life vitally changed—finds himself in union with God. Who is great enough to completely understand these mysteries? It is therefore, as Lewis might say, "mad idolatry"[21] that would replace the Presence with a definition of how it works. Nevertheless definitions are necessary, if not always adequate, and so it is with caution that we approach the meaning of the word "sacrament."

A sacrament is most usually defined as an outward and visible sign of an inward and spiritual grace, a rite which Christ ordained and through which we receive Him, His grace and His gifts. As we have seen, the mediating work of the Holy Spirit is the vital agent in effecting this inward and spiritual grace. It is possible to come to baptism or the Lord's Supper and to perceive nothing but the symbol. One's spirit must be open to the Holy Spirit's work to effectively appropriate the grace which the visible sign represents. To perceive only the symbol is to fail to apprehend the Presence which forms Christ in us, makes us one with our brothers, and grants us Christ's supernatural gifts.

To truly communicate in Holy Communion is to experience Christ, to experience our oneness with God, with our brothers and sisters, and with the saints of every age. This is worship. The experience of true communion can be overpowering. Christ is first apprehended in the preaching of the Word. He is then experienced through the Eucharist. Together both parts achieve a whole: mind, spirit, and body are fed. The absence of a true communion in our worship services is a source of the spiritual malnutrition of our times.

That God does not despise man, that Spirit does indwell matter, was a vital understanding of Paul and the early Christians. "Surely you know that you are God's temple, where the Spirit of God dwells."[22] One writer points out that this saying of Paul's was sheer blasphemy to the Palestinian Jew of the time, regarding as he did the Temple at Jerusalem:

> But it was reasonable to suppose that it was only because St. Paul was convinced by the Spirit, by which every member of the local church had become possessed in

virtue of his initiation, with the mysterious Presence believed to vouchsafe itself within the central Shrine of
Judaism, that he felt able to use this metaphor as he
did.[23]

Similarly, as God is not limited to the temple at
Jerusalem, we cannot limit the channels through
which man "receives" from Him. In his autobiography, *Surprised by Joy,* Lewis describes himself as
the little boy whom God kept calling by sending darts
of Joy into his closed world and as the young pagan to
whom He sent "pictures." *Joy* in Lewis's works has to
do with the Holy Spirit, and with God making Himself known to lost men. And this Joy, full of the divine
Numinous,[24] came to the young Lewis through the
mediums of myth, nature, and Wagnerian music. One
could therefore refer to myth, nature, and music as
"sacramental" in Lewis's case. Even more important
for Lewis, a Christian brother or sister is "sacramental" in the sense that he or she is a channel for that
Presence, a medium through which Love Himself can
flow.

> Next to the Blessed Sacrament itself, your neighbor is the
> holiest object presented to your senses. If he is your
> Christian neighbor he is holy in almost the same way, for
> in him also Christ *vere latitat*—the glorifier and the
> glorified, Glory Himself, is truly hidden.[25]

All things, insofar as they partake of incarnational reality, are potentially sacramental to the ingodded
man.

Finally, Lewis was convinced that no definition, no
explanation, of the sacraments could remove their essential mystery, and he himself refused to attempt any
technical definition:

I do not know and can't imagine what the disciples understood Our Lord to mean when, His body still unbro-
ken and His blood unshed, He handed them the bread
and wine, saying *they* were His body and blood. . . .
And I find "substance" (in Aristotle's sense), when
stripped of its own accidents and endowed with the accidents of some other substance, an object I cannot
think. . . . On the other hand, I get on no better with
those who tell me that the elements are mere bread and
mere wine, used symbolically to remind me of the death
of Christ. They are, on the natural level, such a very odd
symbol of *that*. . . . [I]f they are, if the whole act is, simply memorial, it would seem to follow that its value must
be purely psychological, and dependent on the recipi-
ent's sensibility at the moment of reception. And I cannot see why *this* particular reminder—a hundred other
things may, psychologically, remind me of Christ's
death, equally, or perhaps more—should be so uniquely
important as all Christendom (and my own heart) un-
hesitatingly declare.[26]

That Christ is the mystery to be received, and that His
Presence comes to touch and to heal the believing one
through the sacraments is as far as Lewis is willing to
go toward an explanation. It is here that "the veil between the worlds, nowhere else (for me) so opaque to
the intellect, is nowhere else so thin and permeable to
divine operation. Here a hand from the hidden country touches not only my soul but my body."[27] So
Lewis, lamenting the divisions that the differing definitions had made in the Body of Christ, elected to be
comparatively silent on the sacraments as such. Yet,
since his profoundly holistic view of reality is incarnational, he ends up saying implicitly much more about
sacramental reality than most who address it explicitly.

Whether explicit or implicit, the sacramental view of reality was central to Lewis's thought. He believed in, but also experienced personally, the Real Presence of God—God pouring out His Spirit in and through the material world of His creation, in and through His Church, in and through the holy mysteries of the sacraments. If the Church is to move forward with joy and power in this age she will need to be filled with fresh infusions of God's Spirit, proclaiming and receiving the Real Presence of God in the individual and corporate lives of her members.

4

SPIRIT, SOUL, AND BODY

*"We cannot conceive how the Divine Spirit
dwelled within the human spirit of Jesus:
but neither can we conceive
how His human spirit, or that of any man,
dwells within his natural organism. What we
can understand, if the Christian doctrine
is true, is that our own composite existence
is not the anomaly it might seem to be,
but a faint image of the
Divine Incarnation itself."*
Miracles.

Lewis has been called the apostle to sceptics and
atheists, and this he assuredly is. But he is also (and
perhaps more importantly) the apostle to a Christendom contaminated by a naturalistic view of man
which is hard to distinguish from that of secular
philosophies. Whole aspects of man's being are ig-
nored by Christians intent on nourishing man. Sarah
Smith of Golder's Green, a character in Lewis's *The
Great Divorce*, is a vivid example of what the complete
man is, when fully perfected. She has not been very
well known in her pilgrimage on earth, but fame in
heaven differs from fame as we know it here. And on

this earth Sarah has learned to love. Now, fully infused with the divine life, "Love shone not from her face only, but from all her limbs, as if it were some liquid in which she had just been bathing."[1] As she runs over the green turf on the outskirts of Paradise, "the invitation to all joy" sings "out of her whole being like a bird's song on an April evening."[2] And she is in starkest contrast to the insubstantial and ghostlike "dwarf" whom she has been sent to help. His "other face" or "self" has completely usurped and annihilated the person he could have been, yet the shining clarity of Sarah's own person, as it comes to bear on him, causes even his poor vacant face to become a little clearer. Almost unbearably beautiful, she glows, and the purest love and courtesy flows from her by reason of the radiant substantiveness of her spirit:

> I cannot now remember whether she was naked or clothed. If she were naked, then it must have been the almost visible penumbra of her courtesy and joy which produces in my memory the illusion of a great and shining train that followed her across the happy grass. If she were clothed, then the illusion of nakedness is doubtless due to the clarity with which her inmost spirit shone through the clothes.[3]

Here Lewis has captured the essence of what the perfected self *is*. Sarah Smith's spirit, aglow with the Divine Spirit, illuminates not only her own soul and body but throws forth its beams like liquid gold to encircle and penetrate those who have not yet elected to step into the circle of God's love. And though Sarah Smith of Golder's Green is, admittedly, much "further in and higher up" than those saints who have yet to cross over into the environs of that unmediated and unapproachable Light, even so their faces are intended to shine with this same light of heaven because their spirits are indwelt by Another.[4] This life descending into them recreates them, and they find themselves new-made. Thus transfigured, the life that brings the whole personality into balance is diffused into their rational, intuitive, feeling, sensory, and organic faculties. The Christian view is one of man the creature fully reconciled to God the Creator. To be thus reconciled (healed, restored, forgiven, and loved) is to know the Good. Evil is, as we have seen, separation from God, and psychologically speaking, it is separation within oneself. So the Bright Spirit is not only united to God, it is united within itself. It is redeemed.

Like St. Paul, Lewis describes man as consisting of spirit *(pneuma)*, soul *(psyche)*, and body *(soma)*. Both Plato and Aristotle also understood man as tripartite, but in their systems the mind *(nous,*[5] the principle of intellectual life, reason, and contemplation) is the immortal or spiritual element and the *psyche* is merely the animal soul (the principle of nutritive and sense life), while the *soma* is the material principle in man. There is no equivalent of spirit *(pneuma)* in St. Paul's sense in their systems, and therefore they differ radically from both Paul and Lewis, who understand the spirit to be the highest element in man, rather than the mind or intellect.

In the Christian view the primacy of the spirit is of great importance, as we shall continue to see. Man's spirit answers to the Spirit *(Pneuma)* of God, and when touched by His Spirit becomes from our perspective the Higher Self or the New Man, and from the other perspective (that of the Spirit of God), the Christ formed[6] in us. This highest element in man is thus distinguished from the *psyche* (soul), which Lewis understands to include both the rational soul (the mind, conscious and unconscious, the will, the emotions, the feelings, the imagination, the intuitive faculty), and the animal soul (the instinctual and sensory faculties, *etc.*). Both spirit and soul are then distinguished from the animal body, the *soma* (the body as part of the material world). These three united make up the composite being called man.

Soma, psyche, and *pneuma* each point to a realm of truth, only one of which is effectually acknowledged in higher education today—and that is the truth of *soma* or material nature. This is the realm of the scientist's truth, empirical truth, that can be discerned and measured by the senses. Because this kind of truth is today often understood to be the only one, the present view of man and mind is often reduced to a biological and chemical one.[7]

But besides the truth of nature there are two other kinds which Lewis terms the truth of "Super-Nature" and the truth of "Absolute Being"—that which is "beyond any and every Nature."[8] Lewis not only recognizes the common division between the natural and the supernatural, between that which is "matter" and that which is "spirit," but further distinguishes the uncreated or absolute being of God from the created supernatural. Man, in his body, participates in nature; in his *psyche,* he participates in super-nature; and through his spirit, the whole of him can be linked beyond all nature and super-nature to absolute being.

Super-nature or the supernatural is the realm of supersensory truth in that it is beyond the range of the senses. Like nature, super-nature is still finite, still created. The nonmaterial but created spirits, both good and evil, belong to this realm. Consciousness or the rational soul, the reasoning mind in man, is a part of the super-nature system. The power of reason which is the light of human consciousness becomes incarnate in each human being. Rational thought is therefore not a part of the system of nature but comes down into nature—or, rather, nature is taken up into reason. "We must give up talking about 'human reason.' In so far as thought is merely human . . . it does not explain our knowledge. Where thought is strictly rational it must be, in some odd sense, not ours, but cosmic or super-cosmic."[9]

As part of super-nature incarnate in nature, reason includes not only the thought-process in the individual mind, but objective truth beyond the thinking subject:

> It must be something not shut up inside our heads but already "out there"—in the universe or behind the universe: either as objective as material Nature or more objective still. Unless all that we take to be knowledge is an illusion, we must hold that in thinking we are not reading rationality into an irrational universe but responding to a rationality with which the universe has always been saturated.[10]

For instance, the primary moral principles (the Tao[11] common to all men), called the practical reason, are not only rationally perceived, but are themselves part of reason, which exists objectively in the realm beyond nature. Man, whether pagan or Christian, has access to this truth as a rational creature and can know himself to be a moral and an ethical being as well as an intellectual and a biological one.

Absolute being is, of course, the Reality Who created both nature and super-nature. This Absolute Being is the Spirit beyond or behind the universe

Who is quite beyond man's scientific power of observation. He is a Person, or three Persons in One, Who
created man in His image and Who communicates
Himself to those who will receive Him, thereby redeeming them.

The redeemed man is, in one sense, no different
from the unregenerate man in that he still consists of
the same number of parts or elements—he is still
spirit, soul, and body. Yet, united with that Reality
beyond any and all nature, he is altogether different
now that each part or element is redirected and revitalized.

> [W]hat we are talking about is not (as *soul* and *spirit* are) a
> part or element in Man but a redirection and revitalizing
> of all the parts or elements. Thus in one sense there is
> nothing more in a regenerate man than in an unregener-
> ate man, just as there is nothing more in a man who is
> walking in the right direction than in one who is walking
> in the wrong direction. In another sense, however, it
> might be said that the regenerate man is *totally* different
> from the unregenerate, for the regenerate life, the Christ
> that is formed in him, transforms every part of him: in it
> his spirit, soul and body will all be reborn.[12]

One should point out that for Lewis the sharp division of nature from super-nature, of matter from
created spirit, may be an accident of our limited point
of view. As suggested above (chapter 1), matter and
spirit may be more akin than we know.

The prevailing twentieth-century view of man, unlike the Christian model, is a dreary one indeed. It is
based on the truth of nature alone. Man in this model
is most generally understood as an organism whose
choices are determined by his environment and
heredity, and not as a truly ethical and moral being,

much less one capable of being indwelt by God. Man, along with his world, just sort of "happened,"[13] and his mind (as well as any deity[14] he might admit) simply rose up out of the biological process. He is therefore quite beyond freedom, and he requires not an educator but, quite literally, a conditioner:

> Where the old [education] initiated, the new merely "conditions." The old dealt with its pupils as grown birds deal with young birds when they teach them to fly: the new deals with them more as the poultry-keeper deals with young birds—making them thus or thus for purposes of which the birds know nothing. In a word, the old was a kind of propagation—men transmitting manhood to men: the new is merely propaganda.[15]

Lewis's essay, *The Abolition of Man*, and his novel, *That Hideous Strength*, prophesy quite graphically the logical end of such a view of man. They illustrate the dreadful irony that in his attempt to manipulate nature completely man winds up with no governing values except natural impulse, whim, and caprice. Also, since the desire for the supernatural cannot be completely repressed, dark mysticisms, superstitions, and orgies too dreadful to imagine replace the good of reason, of faith, and even of natural law. As examination of present-day newspapers and magazines will reveal, superstitions and (even dark, perverse) mysticisms void of the truths of nature, reason, and absolute being are already to some extent replacing in the popular mind the materialistic view of man.

The totally natural, even biological, view of man and mind has come about because of a crisis in our understanding of truth. Modern man, having discarded the possibility of supersensory truth, has come to recognize only the truth of the senses. He has come to see himself and his world in terms of only one of the three kinds of truth. He therefore understands and measures himself and everything else only by that one kind. Due to the encroaching uniformity of an ideology that—explicitly or implicitly—would reduce all truth to what can be measured by the senses, our systems of higher education are in a critical stage. As has often been pointed out, man from such a materialistic perspective has no freedom.[16]

The Christian view of man radically differs from the naturalistic view, for the Christian understands himself and his world in the light of the three kinds of truth. A thoroughgoing supernaturalist, the Christian believes that "besides Nature, Something else exists," and that he himself with all nature depends upon this Something else for existence. Unlike the naturalist, who understands himself and his world as a developing (biological and evolutionary) process sufficient and complete in itself, and who explains "the continuity between things that claim to be spiritual and things that are certainly natural by saying that the one slowly turned into the other,"[17] the supernaturalist envisions God coming down into His developed but fallen creation, incarnating it, and coming up again, "pulling it up with Him."[18] The supernaturalist believes that matter can never turn into mind or spirit, but, instead, that matter receives into itself this higher life which is spiritual and supernatural. As Lewis explains:

> We can understand that if God so descends into a human spirit, and human spirit so descends into Nature, and our thoughts into our senses and passions, and if adult minds (but only the best of them) can descend into sympathy with children, and men into sympathy with beasts, then everything hangs together and the total real-

ity, both Natural and Supernatural, in which we are living is more multifariously and subtly harmonious than we had suspected. We catch sight of a new key principle—the power of the Higher, just in so far as it is Higher, to come down, the power of the greater to include the less.[19]

Specifically in regard to unfallen man, the supernaturalist believes that "In perfect cyclic movement, being, power and joy descended from God to man in the form of gift and returned from men to God in the form of obedient love and ecstatic adoration,"[20] and that, in the restoration of man, this is once again the idea, the pattern of man's relationship to ultimate reality.

Unfortunately, however, the mind of Christendom has been contaminated by the naturalistic view of man. The materialistic assumptions in the Christian's unexamined view of himself bar him from miracle, that is, from the supernatural, and from a true understanding of God's Presence without and within. Due to his naturalistic presuppositions, he is no longer free to "listen" to God, to receive His guidance, or to collaborate actively with the Holy Spirit in such a way as to become free from the interior and exterior forces that shape his life and cost him his freedom.

When a proper understanding of the Holy Spirit's work in man is lost, then the Christian, like the materialist, lives solely from the psychological level of his being. He has lost the incarnational way of knowing. His mind, developed apart from an active participation in the Holy Spirit, yields a rationalism that cannot receive spiritual wisdom. Desiring the spiritual experience this rationalism denies him, he may be tempted by occult knowledge, failing to distinguish it

from spiritual wisdom. The imaginative and intuitive
faculty, developed apart from the Holy Spirit's indwelling, can quickly lead into the spuriously spiritual, if not into outright occult bondage. The Christian, laboring under materialistic assumptions concerning his own soul, but hungry in spirit, needs the
intellectual blocks to true spirituality removed—
blocks put there by those of his mentors armed only
with naturalistic presuppositions. He also needs to
understand there are different *kinds* of truth and to
become able to discern and *verbalize* it. While ap-
preciating more than most the truth of the first kind,
the truth of nature, Lewis hands back to the Christian
the knowledge and the *vocabulary* with which to
speak of the supernatural and of absolute being. The
Christian is thus truly *informed*, and not only by the
senses.

We cannot blame only our educational institutions
for this general plight of knowledge, affecting every
quarter: whether Catholic or Protestant, conservative
or liberal, Lewis comments,

> No generation can bequeath to its successor what it has
> not got. You may frame the syllabus as you please. But
> when you have planned and reported *ad nauseam*, if we
> are sceptical we shall teach only scepticism to our pupils,
> if fools only folly, if vulgar only vulgarity, if saints sanc-
> tity, if heroes heroism. Education is only the most fully
> conscious of the channels whereby each generation in-
> fluences the next. It is not a closed system. Nothing
> which was not in the teachers can flow from them into
> the pupils. . . .
> A society which is predominantly Christian will propa-
> gate Christianity through its schools: one which is not, will
> not. All the ministries of education in the world cannot alter

this law. We have, in the long run, little either to hope or fear from government.[21]

Ourselves, rather than our educational systems, are the real problem. When we hear educators or politicians pleading for the restoration of Christian values in the universities or in government, we know their calls are nearly useless because there can be no counteracting trend until the populace itself is converted. Ultimate values are rooted in metaphysical truths, those very truths that we, in our materialistic society, have lost. *Therefore our hope is not in calling for our systems to be Christian, but in becoming truly Christian ourselves.*

In becoming truly Christian we become truly free. Because the Christian understands a Mind outside of nature, guiding both himself and his cosmos, he has no fear of contingency or of fate and mere circumstance, in regard either to the cosmos or himself. He believes that the Uncreated Who comes down is the Good, and that in Him is no darkness nor shadow of turning, and that this Good is "not simply a law, but also a begetting Love." Therefore he believes in meaningful freedom rather than in chance or fate. In fact, the Christian believes he was created precisely so that he could be free and therefore able to love, and that this same begetting Love indwelling him is capable of lifting him out of the cauldron of predetermined fate and of resurrecting him in every part of his being. Like that Bright Spirit, Sarah Smith of Golder's Green, he is enabled to radiate this freedom to other spirits yet in bondage. Such is the fully restored Christian view of man.

5
TILL WE HAVE FACES

*"God came first in his [Adam's] love
and in his thought,
and that without painful effort.
In perfect cyclic movement, being, power and
joy descended from God to man in the form
of gift and returned from man
to God in the form of obedient love and
ecstatic adoration . . ."*
The Problem of Pain.

*"And Adam and Eve hid themselves
from the presence of the Lord God amongst
the trees of the Garden."*
Genesis 3:8.

Something far more basic than modern man's materialism works against a true knowledge of himself and his condition—the Fall and its effects. As Lewis's great mythic work *Till We Have Faces* dramatically illustrates, the fallen self cannot know itself. Orual, Queen of the ancient pagan kingdom of Glome, picks up her pen to write her case against the gods, and she bitterly complains that they do not answer her cries. In her first book she tells her life-story, a tale full of anguish and loss. In it she realizes that the real Orual has escaped into 'the queen': "I locked Orual up or laid her asleep as best I could somewhere deep inside me. . . . It was like being with child, but reversed; the thing I carried in me grew slowly smaller and less alive."[1]

Escaping into queenship, she became a great queen, and the best ruler in the history of her little barbarous kingdom. One of her great strengths lay in the fact that she wore a veil to hide her ugliness. Although even as a child she had been fiercely ugly, she did not don her veil until after she had hidden from her friend Lysias her first glimpse of the truth about the gods—that they are really beautiful and good. Lysias (nicknamed the Fox) was a Greek slave who had not only taught her his rationalistic philosophy but had been one of only three persons she had (or thought she had) really loved. The other two were her half-sister, Psyche, and her trusted warrior, Bardia. Beneath her veil, she became an exceedingly strong ruler, but on leaving her Pillar Room and her subjects for the night, she would go to her own bed chamber—there to find herself alone with her "nothingness."

Vying always with the rationalist teachings of the Fox for the mind of Orual was the dark, bloody religion of the awful idol goddess named Ungit and her cultic priests. Ungit was a shapeless stone over which blood sacrifices were poured. Orual says of her that she had no face but later explains that for Ungit to have no face only means "she had a thousand faces." Since early childhood Orual had been dreadfully afraid of the Priest of Ungit and of the "Ungit smell" that accompanied him. It was a temple-smell of blood to her. Sometimes he sacrificed men too. Burnt fat and singed hair and stale incense made up the Ungit smell—the smell of "holiness."

There came a time when this priest required Orual's sister Psyche, the person she loved more than all else in the world, as a sacrifice to Ungit. In ending her book of complaint against the gods, she cries out, "They gave me nothing in the world to love but Psyche and then took her away from me." Asking the question, "Why must holy places be dark places?" she challenges the gods: "I say, therefore, that there is no creature (toad, scorpion, or serpent) so noxious to man as the gods. Let them answer my charge if they can."

Orual, thinking her case against the gods to be finished, rolled up her scroll only to find she must unroll it and write yet another book. In this one she says, "What began the change was the very writing itself," for after setting down her charges, Orual was "drenched with seeings." In dreams, visions, and by various circumstances, Orual was shown her real self. Realizing that even her love for Psyche, Bardia, and the Fox was a selfish thing, she is forced to cry out, "I am Ungit." She saw that her Kingdom, Glome, was a web and that she herself was "the swollen spider, squat at its center, gorged with men's stolen lives."

At last in a vision she is sent as a prisoner of Ungit down into the deadlands, there to stand on trial before the tens of thousands of the dead, including the old King her father and the Fox and others she had known in life. Here she finds herself not only unveiled, but stripped naked, and in her hands she holds the complaint she has written against the gods. When she begins to read it aloud before that awful assembly, however, she finds it not to be her book at all. It is instead the true tale of her life. It ends this way:

"I know what you'll say. You will say the real gods are not at all like Ungit, and that I was shown a real god . . . and ought to know it! Hypocrites! I do know it. . . . Do you think the mortals will find you gods easier to bear if you're beautiful? . . . We want to be our own."[2]

Her judge in this awful scene has a veil on, and Orual finds that she is actually her own judge, for her complaint turns out to be the answer she is seeking. "I saw well why the gods do not speak to us openly. . . . How can they meet us face to face till we have faces?"

Orual's essential self or spirit had fallen deep into the dark labyrinth of her own lost soul; she could not know that self yet she rejected every glimpse of another more lovely reality outside that self. In her first book she appears to be excruciatingly honest, even to herself. But it is, as Lewis says, hard for the fallen self to tell the tale the way it really is: "I do not think it is our fault that we cannot tell the truth about ourselves; the persistent, lifelong, inner murmur of spite, jealousy, prurience, greed and self-complacence, simply will not go into words."[3]

Moreover, it is the plight of the human spirit which is no longer master of its own soul and body to be severely limited. The intellect is affected by a corruption of the spirit that has turned from God to its self. The fallen will cooperates with an imagination filled with shapes that cater to its own spiritual and physical lusts. The intuitive faculty can be described as often paranoid, both toward God and toward one's neighbors. One's emotions and feelings support only too well that which calls one to separate from, and refuse to harmonize with, the Holy Other and with the shining realities outside oneself.

In other books Lewis describes the darts of sheer Joy

that eventually caused him to know there was an Other—to know there was One Who was outside and separate from himself and Who was calling to him. Orual is really Lewis, and her tale is not only his but it is the story of all men: it is the story of the old Adamic self, faceless (or having a thousand faces) and fallen from the Presence.

Adam, unfallen, had no identity problem. He was a creature in communion with the Life-Giver. As a single flower opens broadfaced to receive its life from the sun, so Adam lifted his face and received joy, power, his very being, from God. In his disobedience and resulting Fall, Adam's relationship to God was broken. Once he and Eve, as creatures, ceased to direct every aspect of their lives to the Creator, they lost wholeness and became sick in spirit (the essential self), in soul (mind, will, and emotions), in body, and in all their exterior relationships. Indeed, they no longer knew God, themselves, or others:

> Thus human spirit from being the master of human nature became a mere lodger in its own house, or even a prisoner; rational consciousness became what it now is—a fitful spot-light resting on a small part of the cerebral motions. But this limitation of the spirit's powers was a lesser evil than the corruption of the spirit itself. It had turned from God and become its own idol, so that though it could still turn back to God, it could do so only by painful effort, and its inclination was self-ward. Hence pride and ambition, the desire to be lovely in its own eyes and to depress and humiliate all rivals, envy, and restless search for more, and still more, security, were now the attitudes that came easiest to it.[4]

Christ commanded and empowered His followers to heal because He knew that all men, in their exterior relationships and within themselves, are broken and separated. In order for man to regain wholeness in every aspect of his life, the relationships between himself and God, himself and other men, himself and nature, and himself and his innermost being, must be healed. And this healing must include the will, the unconscious mind or the deep heart, the emotions, and the intuitive and imaginative faculties. The key to the healing of all these relationships has to do with incarnational reality—with being filled with God's Spirit and with seeking to dwell in His Presence. It has to do with man's choosing union and communion with God rather than his own separateness which is, in effect, the "practice of the presence" of the old Adamic fallen self. To be filled with the Spirit is to choose the heaven of the integrated and emancipated self rather than the hell of the disintegrated self in separation. It is to choose the same love that has bound together the Father and the Son throughout all eternity. It is to enter the Great Dance of healthy relationship with the self, others, God, and His creation.

"Blessed," said our Lord, "are the poor in spirit." Blessed, indeed are those who know how poor and empty, apart from their Lord's indwelling, they truly are. On the other hand, in union with Christ, men are "God's work of art, created in Christ to live the good life as from the beginning he had meant us to live it."[5] This work of art is the believer, one who in union with Christ has found his "higher self," and consequently has a real "I" or face with which to meet and commune, however humbly, with God. About this relationship Lewis exclaimed: "To be loved by God, not merely pitied, but delighted in as an artist delights in his work or a father in a son—it seems impossible, a weight or burden of glory which our thoughts can hardly sustain."[6] To be thus molded by the Creator is to find that heaven, though yet unattained, is retroactive, working backwards into our existence and turning even our earthly sufferings into glory.[7]

In ceasing to direct her every action and thought to her Creator, Eve displayed the self-will which, as Lewis says, is the only sin conceivable as the Fall. Her self-will was, in effect, a denial of her creaturehood. The created finite would contend with the Uncreated Infinite. Such pride cannot be rationally comprehended but can be well enough recognized, since we all experience it.

> From the moment a creature becomes aware of God as God and of itself as self, the terrible alternative of choosing God or self for the centre is opened to it. This sin is committed daily by young children and ignorant peasants as well as by sophisticated persons, by solitaries no less than by those who live in society: it is the fall in every individual life, and in each day of each individual life, the basic sin behind all particular sins: at this very moment you and I are either committing it, or about to commit it, or repenting it.[8]

Christ has commanded His disciples to be healers of the spirits, souls, and bodies of men, for we all have cut ourselves off from the very source of life. To look upward toward God in this condition is to show many faces. Masks, in fact, are required that we might hide from the Presence as our first parents hid behind leaves. The real "I," buried deeply in layers of the self, must be sovereignly resurrected if it is to find its one true face with which to meet the Presence.

Christ came to free man from the bondage of the false self, and He found that "The Spirit of the Lord is upon me, because he has anointed me to preach good

news to the poor."[7] Even as Christ collaborated with
the Spirit of the Lord to free man from the hell of
self-will and pride, so His disciples are commanded to
do the same. We proclaim liberty to the captives, freedom to the prisoners. We call forth, in the name of
Christ, the real person. This is what being a disciple
is; this is what "carrying the cross" is all about. And,
it is always God's Presence that heals, that calls the
higher self into being. Apart from Him we have no
higher self. We are many-selved, many-faced.

We must therefore open every door of our being to
this Presence, to our God. It is then that we are healed
in spirit, in intellect and will, and in our intuitive,
imaginative, and sensory faculties. And it is then that
we as healers, as channels of God's Love and Presence, literally carry Christ into the lives of others.
Christ's aim is to fill the whole life of the believer.
That is what conversion is—the ongoing process of
being filled with Christ. The Holy Spirit, truly present
and operative in the human spirit, is capable of resurrecting every faculty of man. It is from this healing
Presence, this gracious flow of life and power, that
Adam and Eve fell.

The unfallen Adam and Eve could hear God—and
they could listen to Him. They had union and communion with the Life-Giver. They were, in other
words, God-conscious and not self-conscious. They
had eyes that could see clearly because their motives
were single. They had one face that could look up at
the sound of the voice of God. Their spirits were alive;
they therefore had authority over all nature, including
their own souls and bodies. Their souls (psychological
faculties), under the control of a spirit that was indwelt by God, yielded what could be called a holy
intellect, a creative, richly producing imaginative fac-

ulty, a healthy and wholesome and richly informing intuitive faculty, and a will without blemish. Their sensory, emotional, and feeling faculties were in harmonious accord with the Spirit of God and with all nature. Their minds contained no memories, conscious or unconscious, to remind them of their need for forgiveness or a need to forgive others. They had no horror of themselves such as we call, in the jargon of today, a "bad self-image." Their thoughts and ideas were not based on, or cluttered by, false ideologies or misplaced loyalties. They had no repressed desires, no memories of maltreatment, and no experiences of rejection by others.

They had received only love. Their relationships with God, with each other, and with the animal kingdom around them were relationships of love. They were channels of love to all creation. There is no doubt they blessed all they touched. Experiencing always the Real Presence of God, love flowed out from them; they were Sons of God who did not know separation from God.

Orual, Queen of Glome and fallen daughter of Eve, had known nothing more than separateness. There came a time, however, when "drenched with seeings," she was brought to the side of a pool and felt the presence of a god coming to judge her. The very air seemed to be set on fire at this approach, and she found herself pierced through and through with joy and sweetness. She, the fiercely ugly one, was unmade, and was no one. But presently, looking into the pool, she found herself not only clothed—but beautiful. Orual, now able to hear the Voice speaking to her and calling her by her new name, cried: "I ended my first book with the words *no answer.* I know now,

Lord, why you utter no answer. You are yourself the answer."[10] Ultimate Truth is a Person, a Real Presence. Orual now had a face, a real "I"; cleansed, she had come into that Presence. Though presented in the form of an epic myth, Lewis was expressing a universal truth: man will find his true self only in communion and union with Christ—only through experiencing the Real Presence of God, reconciling man to himself, to his Creator, and to the created world.

6

WE'VE BEEN "UNDRAGONED"

*"[T]hat is enough to raise our thoughts
to what may happen when the redeemed soul,
beyond all hope and nearly beyond
belief, learns at last that she has pleased Him
whom she was created to please. There
will be no room for vanity then. She will be
free from the miserable illusion that
it was all her doing. With no taint of what
we should now call self-approval she
will most innocently rejoice in the thing
that God has made her to be, and the
moment which heals her old inferiority
complex will also drown her pride deeper
than Prospero's book. Perfect humility
dispenses with modesty."*
"Weight of Glory," Weight of Glory.

Lewis realized that if we are not to spend our lives like
Orual in isolating the self and building "a case against
the gods," radical surgery is necessary. This radical
surgery will restore our true face, our true self, though
the perfecting of that self will take more than a lifetime. In order for this surgery to occur, we must die to
the old self with Christ, and be born anew into Him.

Like Eustace in *The Voyage of the Dawn Treader*[1] we
must be "undragoned."

Eustace is a greedy boy who, caring only for "facts,"
has never been to the country of Narnia. The reality of
Narnia doesn't fit his idea of "facts." He has overheard his cousins, the Pevenses, talking about their
secret country, and thereafter loves to tease and bully
them about their belief. He never believes that they
have *really* been there. But one day, along with his
cousins, he is suddenly "pulled" into Narnia through
a painting of a ship under full sail. Being tossed into a
Narnian sea and hauled up into a Narnian boat is
about the worst thing that could happen to the selfish
Eustace, for he lands right in the middle of people
who have learned long ago that it isn't a joyful thing to
be selfish. And their joy and unselfishness puts him
out of sorts.

One day an even more dreadful thing happens to
him: "Sleeping on a dragon's hoard with greedy,
dragonish thoughts in his heart, he had become a dragon himself."[2] A dragon is not only a selfish monster
that hoards treasures, but it is also a very lonely creature. One cause of its loneliness is that it likes nothing
better to eat than fresh dragon as well as other animals
and human beings. Eustace begins to experience how
lonely it is to be a monster. He begins to realize what
kind of person he has been. And as the full realization
of this settles upon him, the dragon who is Eustace
lifts up his awful dragon head and begins to weep.

Through his tears he sees a huge and awesome Lion
come toward him and beckon him to follow. So great
is Eustace's loneliness by this time that he will do
anything that Great Beast asks. The Lion leads him to
a huge, round well, and there he directs Eustace to
undress. Eustace has on no clothes but he then re-

members that dragons are rather like snakes, and he
thinks perhaps he can shed his awful dragon hide. He
starts scratching away at his scaly self and soon man-
ages to step right out of his dragon suit. But just as he
steps into the water, he notices he has yet a smaller
dragon skin on underneath. Once again he scratches
away at this hide, and stepping out of it, starts again
into the water. But there again he sees he is still a
dragon. He thinks to himself, " 'Oh dear, how ever
many skins have I got to take off?' "[3] He then scratches
away for the third time and is almost desperate to find
he has yet another dragon skin on. It is then that the
Lion says, "You will have to let me undress you."
Eustace is dreadfully afraid of the Lion's claws, but he
is desperate by then, so he lays down his ugly
dragon-self and lets the Lion undress him. The very
first tear that the Lion's claws make goes so deep that
Eustace thinks it has gone right through his heart and
hurts worse than anything he has ever felt.

Then Aslan catches hold of him with his great,
clawed paws and throws him into the crystal-clear
pool. And, smarting terribly at first, Eustace the dragon sinks deep into the delicious waters until, surfac-
ing, he finds himself turned back into a boy.

Few, if any, write better than Lewis of our need to
be "undragoned." Like Eustace, he saw with terrible
clarity that our conversion from loving self to loving
God and our neighbors is a radical one indeed. Because of Lewis's profound understanding of the old,
fallen self, some thought that he had studied moral or
ascetic theology for years. Refusing the compliment,
he replied, "They forgot that there is an equally reliable, though less creditable, way of learning how
temptation works. 'My heart'—I need no other's—
'showeth me the wickedness of the ungodly.' "[4]

A good number of years before he penned those words, at a time when he was first attempting obedience but before his conversion to Christ,[5] he wrote to his life-long friend, Arthur Greeves, and told of what he was beginning to find in his heart:

What worries me much more is *pride*—my besetting sin, as yours is *indolence*. During my afternoon "meditations"—which I at least *attempt* quite regularly now—I have found out ludicrous and terrible things about my own character. Sitting by, watching the rising thoughts to break their necks as they pop up, one learns to know the sort of thoughts that do come. And, will you believe it, one out of every three is a thought of self-admiration: when everything else fails, having had its neck broken, up comes the thought "What an admirable fellow I am to have broken their necks!" I catch myself posturing before the mirror, so to speak, all day long. I pretend I am carefully thinking out what to say to the next pupil (for *his* good, of course) and then suddenly realize I am really thinking how frightfully clever I'm going to be and how he will admire me. I pretend I am remembering an evening of good fellowship in a really friendly and charitable spirit—and all the time I'm really remembering how good a fellow I am and how well I talked. And then when you free yourself to stop it, you admire yourself for doing *that*. It's like fighting the hydra (you remember, when you cut off one head another grew). There seems to be no end to it. Depth under depth of self-love and self-admiration. Closely connected with this is the difficulty I find in making even the faintest approach to giving up my own will: which as everyone has told us is the only thing to do.[6]

This revelation continued as Lewis, incredibly honest both with himself and others, saw into the depths of his being the animal and the diabolic selves con-

tending with his human self.[7] He came to understand
the "old self" to be that which would love itself with
partiality or even to the exclusion of all other selves,[8]
and, endeavoring to "die" to that "old self," he
pressed on into Christ and into Joy.

Clyde S. Kilby has said that never since John the
Revelator has anyone written so well about joy as
Lewis has.[9] Most readers of Lewis would agree, and
there is a reason why this should be so. Lewis had, I
believe, such a vivid revelation of joy and the freedom
of the liberated soul precisely because his comprehen-
sion of the hell and the bondage of the fallen self had
been so great. Yet—and this is important to the understanding of Lewis's image of man—along with the
hell he found in the human heart were also "radiant
things, delights and inspirations";[10] he saw that they,
as well as the animal and diabolical selves, surface to
face the living God. And this is, among other reasons,
why he disbelieved the doctrine of the total depravity
of man: "I disbelieve that doctrine, partly on the logical ground that if our depravity were total we should
not know ourselves to be depraved, and partly because experience shows us much goodness in human
nature."[11] Also, it seemed to him that this doctrine
inculcated in its adherents an emotional view[12] of the
self that in the long run impeded a wholesome understanding of it. This inculcated state of feeling toward
oneself could even become a substitute for, or barrier
against, receiving the real grace of God, and thereby
the healing knowledge of the higher self. For instance,
Lewis stressed the act of confession and the reception
of pardon as a most important and objective act, and
was on his guard against those "states of feeling" that
would make of this important act a merely subjective
thing. It seemed to him that a "programme of perma-

nent emotions"[13] about ourselves could turn even the act of our confession into a mere state of "feeling" about ourselves.

He therefore stands apart from that particular school of thought that would include, as an "essential symptom of the regenerate life" a "permanent, and permanently horrified, perception of one's natural and (it seems) unalterable corruption."[14] Lewis certainly had seen his own " 'inward and original corruption' and those 'slimy things that crawled with legs' in his own dungeon," yet he felt it was a great mistake to make of this, as some would, "not a glimpse but a daily life-long scrutiny." He would replace this scrutiny with an understanding of the indwelling Christ, and he came to prefer the practice of this Presence rather than that of the old, carnal man. He believed this was in accord with the Scriptures. To perceive, always and at all times, one's natural corruption seemed "unlike the New Testament fruits of the Spirit—love, joy, and peace. And very unlike the Pauline programme; 'forgetting those things which are behind and reaching forth unto those things that are before.' "[15]

Besides that objection, he found that his feelings (the degrees of shame and disgust he felt) did not at all correspond to what his reason told him of the gravity of his sins. This is only one example of what Lewis constantly points out as the dangers of introspection and of dwelling on the subjective at the expense of the objective. The objective deals with the reality itself;[16] the subjective deals with our sensations or feelings *about* reality, the impressions or track that the reality imprints as it descends into our sensory or feeling beings. To introspectively dwell on "feelings" within oneself is a subjectivism that in worship or prayer leads away from the higher reality of God's objective presence and to the lower reality of our own psychic and sensory beings. This subjectivism obscures, in the case of confession and the ensuing reception of God's pardon, the very grace, joy, and peace mediated by the Holy Spirit, and therefore the reality of God's forgiveness. The guilt therefore remains in the unconscious. This, of course, destroys rather than builds up the spiritual life. Lewis discovered this principle only after introspection had ruined his prayer-life as a child and later threatened to destroy his imaginative life.

[A]s a schoolboy, I had destroyed my religious life by a vicious subjectivism which made "realizations" the aim of prayer; turning away from God to seek states of mind, and trying to produce those states of mind by "maistry." With unbelievable folly I now proceeded to make exactly the same blunder in my imaginative life; or rather the same pair of blunders. The first was made at the very moment when I formulated the complaint that the "old thrill" was becoming rarer and rarer. For by that complaint I smuggled in the assumption that what I wanted was a "thrill," a state of my own mind. And there lies the deadly error. Only when your whole attention and desire are fixed on something else—whether a distant mountain, or the past, or the gods of Asgard—does the "thrill" arise. It is a by-product. Its very existence presupposes that you desire not it but something other and outer.[17]

In regard to our religious life, there are two things to be especially noted: first of all, our emotional or sensory reactions to our behavior is of limited ethical significance. To repent and to turn from sin and the self is a matter of the will, not the feelings. Second, and most important, we can, by substituting for reality our feelings or states of mind, miss the Reality Himself.

The act of penitence and the reception of pardon are definite acts—a very real transaction with God, and we fail in this when we turn from God to seek feelings or states of our own minds. In Lewis's case, though the guilt was real, he found it was removed not by looking inward but by looking outward. It is when man looks up to Jesus that he finds the road out of the self. To take one's eyes off the reality of the Creator and to cast them instead onto the creature is to find oneself again in bondage.[18] In the case of one's imaginative life, it is easy to see how this same kind of blunder is made. When the aesthetic "thrill" becomes the goal, one has lost sight of the objects outside oneself that would, or could, evoke this state of being. A substitute has replaced the reality.

The whole dialectic of desire and the theme of longing in Lewis has to do with this very thing. Man is not the center, though he has made himself to be. But there is within him that desire for heaven and for reality. And this thing that is longed for summons him up and away from the self. He is there united with that hitherto "unattainable ecstasy" that has always hovered just beyond the reach of the fallen soul, and he is therefore forgiven, and released from his guilt. And it is this one who is coming into harmony with God, with others, within himself—in other words, it is the one who is being healed in the inner man—who understands most clearly the evil still left in him. He need not dwell on it as it surfaces; he need only repent of it:

> When a man is getting better, he understands more and more clearly the evil that is still left in him. When a man is getting worse, he understands his own badness less and less. A moderately bad man knows he is not very

good: a thoroughly bad man thinks he is all right.[19]

We see that, in a manner of speaking, it takes a good person to repent, a totally depraved one could not:

> Since I have begun to pray, I find my extreme view of personality changing. My own empirical self is becoming more and more important, and this is the opposite of self-love. You don't teach a seed how to die into treehood by throwing it into the fire: and it has to become a good seed before it's worth burying.[20]

One's conversion does not guarantee, however, that a soul will continue to progress in its imitation of Christ. There is always the matter of resisting temptation and of struggling against the pride and spiritual ignorance of one's heart. Being a Christian can, if it doesn't make one a great deal better, make one a great deal worse:

> For the Supernatural, entering a human soul, opens to it new possibilities both of good and evil. From that point the road branches: one way to sanctity, humility, the other to spiritual pride, self-righteousness, persecuting zeal. And no way back to the mere humdrum virtues of the unawakened soul. If the Divine call does not make us better, it will make us very much worse. Of all bad men religious bad men are the worst.[21]

Pride is the great sin, the one which leads to every other vice, and it can crop up in the redeemed with far more disastrous results than in the unregenerate. The unregenerate self is one that wills to be separate, to be autonomous, to put itself first. The same free will that makes such an evil possible in the first place can, at any stage of the spiritual life, cease to choose the good and again choose itself. John, in Pilgrim's Regress, finds himself dying many deaths, and learns that this dying is the only escape from Death.[22] Our escape from Death consists largely in our learning to die daily to the "old man" and in regular acts of repentance followed by receptions of God's forgiveness.

Repentance and the reception of God's forgiveness, far from a set of emotions or feelings about oneself, is a definite act, a healing transaction between man and God. The need for this act, no matter in what stage of the spiritual journey one finds himself, never lessens. The seasoned saint, no less than the initiate, needs this frequent exercise. Furthermore, this exercise should form a pattern woven into the ongoing spiritual life. This pattern is necessary because, though there may be no conscious awareness of sin, there is always that within us which the Christ-life would heal and forgive. We need to reserve a special time, preferably before receiving Communion, to be deeply quiet before the Lord and to ask Him to descend into our "deep heart," our unconscious, and to bring up those things that are displeasing to Him. It is, as Lewis's writings so well express, perfectly amazing what He brings up to our conscious minds. We then confess these things specifically, avoiding generalities as far as possible, as well as any justifications we might be tempted to make. We can have, as Lewis suggests,[23] pen and paper ready to record any sin that is brought to our conscious minds. We then simply confess it, and, as a definite act, receive forgiveness. This is not introspection: this is our interaction with God, and it constitutes a definite act of the Holy Spirit in our lives. We must, of course, be careful to forgive others, and to release any resentment or bitterness that we have against those who have injured either ourselves or those we love. Also, there are times when apologies and reparations are in order.

But the point to be stressed is, these *are* definite acts, part of a rhythm to be built into our lives. This interaction with God, with our fellow man, and with those things within ourselves is not to be replaced by a permanent, daily, and lifelong scrutiny and horror of the self. Such would constitute a practice of the presence of the "old man" and fail to comprehend the presence of the new man or the higher self. We are therefore careful to rise up out of the depths of confession and of our posture as repentant sinner into the joy and power of the forgiven child of God. Our prime identity is that of a child of God, and we exult in our forgiven and redeemed state.

Part of Lewis's spiritual strength came from the fact that he wove into the busy schedule of his life the pattern of a monthly confession made to a "wise old clergyman."[24] As an Anglican, he was familiar with the exhortation that follows the Communion Service:

> If there be any of you who by this means [of self-examination, repentance, reception of Holy Communion for the forgiveness of sins] cannot quiet his own conscience herein, but requireth further comfort or counsel, let him come to me [the priest], or to some other Minister of God's Word, and open his grief.[25]

And Lewis had grief—memories from throughout his lifetime—that needed the healing that comes through God's forgiveness. In *Letters to Malcolm* he seems to be alluding to one major healing in his own life. He writes about forgiving "someone I have been trying to forgive for over thirty years," and of his discovery that "forgiving (that man's cruelty) and being forgiven (my resentment) were the very same thing."[26] This exchange refers, most likely, to the fiendish and almost insane schoolmaster, "Oldie," under whose roof Lewis had the misfortune both to live and be tutored. But an even greater blot on his conscience and memory, and one he was most ashamed of, was his past attitudes and feelings toward his own father. He considered these to constitute the darkest chapter in his life, and for forgiveness of them he often prayed. I would suggest that it is the healing of this deep remorse to which he makes reference in the following letter to his friend and confidante, Sr. Penelope:

> As for me I specially need your prayers because I am (like the pilgrims in Bunyan) travelling across "a plain called Ease." Everything without, and many things within are marvellously well at present: Indeed . . . I realize that until about a month ago I never really believed (tho' I thought I did) in God's forgiveness. What an ass I have been both for not knowing and for thinking I knew. I now feel that one must never say one believes or understands anything; any morning a doctrine I thought I already possessed may blossom into this new reality.[27]

His insights into prayer and into the reception of forgiveness did indeed blossom after this time and he was enabled to write the book on prayer that he had before attempted, only to put it away.

Lewis's experience is a good example of a grief that needs to be confessed to a priest or minister who can in turn pronounce the forgiveness of Christ, and in such a way that the deep heart (or the unconscious mind) can receive it. Lewis realized the value of this act as it has been worked out in the Church, and therefore he took advantage of the Confessional or the Sacrament of Penance, and of regular Communion.

Lewis also came to understand, with great clarity, that "all times are eternally present to God,"[28] and he laboured to dispel our strange illusions about time and forgiveness. He understood how the divine forgiveness, the eternal efficacy of the work Christ accomplished in Gethsemane and on the Cross, works all the way backward in time to the first man, Adam, and all the way forward to the last man who will ever be born:

> We have a strange illusion that mere time cancels sin. I have heard others, and I have heard myself, recounting cruelties and falsehoods committed in boyhood as if they were no concern of the present speaker's, and even with laughter. But mere time does nothing either to the fact or to the guilt of a sin. The guilt is washed out not by time but by repentance and the blood of Christ.[29]

Lewis therefore understood how God, outside of time, heals our oldest and deepest sorrows. By our repentance and the shedding of His Blood, Christ walks back in time as we know it, forgiving our sins and healing our sorrows, so that we may find wholeness. "To be God is to enjoy an infinite present where nothing has yet passed away and nothing is still to come."[30] To be Christian man is to experience the healing Christ as He walks back in time and forgives our blackest sins and heals our deepest hurts. Furthermore, we find that His Presence was there all along had we only known it, and we merely appropriate the Love that had even then, at the very moment, been there. For years Lewis had not been able to forgive himself for his failure to love his father, nor had he been able to appropriate God's forgiveness for this sin. But when finally enabled he was almost incredulous of the peace and the ease he experienced. This is

the heritage of the sons of God, this is the peace promised by Jesus Christ; and, when it is received, it floods
the finite soul—the dweller in chaotic time.

It is possible, once we have begun on the road to
sanctity and humility, to forget whence we have
come. Eustace, after being delivered from his awful
misery, wondered if it had all been a bad dream. He
wondered if he had really been a scaly dragon and if
Aslan had really taken him up from the pool and dressed him. His friend, Edmund, remembering the old
Eustace, quickly assured him that he really had been a
dragon. To walk successfully this road we must never
forget that we have been "undragoned." But neither
must we forget that, through pride and self-will, we
can once again cater to that old nature.

The most important thing is to *keep on,* not to be discour-
aged however often one yields to the temptation, but
always to pick yourself up again and ask forgiveness. In
reviewing your sins don't either exaggerate them or
minimize them. Call them by their ordinary names and
try to see them as you w[oul]d see the same faults in
somebody else—no special blackening or whitewashing.
Remember the conditions on which we are promised
forgiveness: we shall always be forgiven provided that
we forgive all who sin against us. If we do that we have
nothing to fear: if we don't, all else will be in vain. Of
course there are other helps which are mere common
sense. We must learn by experience to avoid either trains
of thought or social situations which *for us* (not necessarily for everyone) lead to temptations, like motoring—
don't wait until the last moment before you put on the
brakes but put them on, gently and quietly, while the
danger is still a good way off.[31]

It is only by remembering that "Another lives in me"

that we can die daily to that old, false, usurping self, and that we continue to be drawn "further in and higher up" into the life of God. To "practice the Presence" is to call to mind, continually, this great reality. Lewis writes of this Reality Whose presence we are to practice as it is experienced in Christian prayer:

> The thing that matters is being actually drawn into that three-personal life. . . .
>
> An ordinary, simple Christian kneels down to say his prayers. He is trying to get in touch with God. But if he is a Christian he knows that what is prompting him to pray is also God: God, so to speak, inside him. But he also knows that all his real knowledge of God comes through Christ, the Man who was God—that is Christ standing beside him, helping him to pray, praying for him. You see what is happening. God is the thing to which he is praying—the goal he is trying to reach. God is also the road or bridge along which he is pushed to that goal. . . . [T]he whole threefold life of the three-personal Being is actually going on in that ordinary little bedroom where an ordinary man is saying his prayers. The man is being caught up into the higher kind of life—what I call *Zoe* or spiritual life: he is being pulled into God, by God, while still remaining himself.[32]

Once again we see that the secret is incarnational. One dies to the old self and lives to the new by continuing to receive of that Other Life. Even our prayers, in true prayer, are really His prayers. He speaks to Himself through us. And it is the same with all the virtues and all the fruits and gifts of the Spirit. All are equally derivative. We must never forget this, and we must practice, always, this Holy Presence, even though "we can do it only for moments at first":

That is why the real problem of the Christian life comes

where people do not usually look for it. It comes the very moment you wake up each morning. All your wishes and hopes for the day rush at you like wild animals. And the first job each morning consists in shoving them all back; in listening to that other voice, taking that other point of view, letting that other larger, stronger, quieter life come flowing in. . . .

We can do it [practice the Presence] only for moments at first. But from those moments the new sort of life will be spreading through our systems because now we are letting Him work at the right part of us.[33]

And, as Lewis says, "This is the whole of Christianity. There is nothing else."[34] Christianity isn't a covenant or a law but it is a life—it is Another Life being lived in and through us. Our human spirit, when in union with this Holy Other, *is* the higher self. The "practice of the Presence" leads to the knowledge of this higher self, and away from either the wrong kind of self-love or self-hatred. It is in this New Life that we find our souls as well as our spirits—indeed, the whole of our nature—raised. This is why, "Where other systems expose our total nature to death . . . Christianity demands only that we set right a *misdirection* of our nature, and has no quarrel, like Plato, with the body as such, nor with the psychical elements in our makeup."[35] We do not fear our intellects, our imaginations, our emotions, our intuitive beings, our bodies. We simply offer them wholly to God and find them revitalized and redirected. By the principle of the incarnation the Highest is transposed into the lowest and man finds himself resurrected in every faculty of his being. This is the true, the whole self:

At the beginning I said there were Personalities in God. I will go further now. There are no real personalities anywhere else. Until you have given up your self to Him you will not have a real self. Sameness is to be found most among the most "natural" men, not among those who surrender to Christ. How monotonously alike all the great tyrants and conquerors have been: how gloriously different are the saints.[36]

7

THE GREAT DANCE

*"Obedience and rule are more like a dance
than a drill."*
That Hideous Strength.

*"You do not fail in obedience through lack of
love, but have lost love because you never
attempted obedience."*
That Hideous Strength.

By attempting obedience, Orual in *Till We Have Faces*,
walked into the presence of the One whom she had
long denied. In the reality of that Presence she was
unmade, and found herself to be no one. This is the
very experience Lewis had. He tells us that when he
first seriously attempted to obey his conscience[1] he
found himself struggling with a "Spirit" or a "Real I"
who, unlike the "god" of his philosophical Idealism
was "showing an alarming tendency to become much
more personal and is taking the offensive, and behav-
ing just like God."[2] And it was in this "Real Presence"
that he first knew himself to be no one:

[P]resently you begin to wonder whether you are yet, in
any full sense, a person at all; whether you are entitled to

call yourself "I" (it is a sacred name). . . . You find that
what you called yourself is only a thin film on the surface
of an unsounded and dangerous sea. But not merely
dangerous. Radiant things, delights and inspirations,
come to the surface as well as snarling resentments and
nagging lusts. One's ordinary self is, then, a mere facade.
There's a huge area out of sight behind it.[3]

So it was that as Lewis discovered God to be no
impersonal force that he also found his view of human
personality changed. Each man's personality is di-
vided within him and needs to become one before he
can know who he is. Lewis saw that whatever else is
involved, finally our *human will* determines whether
or not our personality is made one. He expresses this
insight in terms of Christ's soul: "This human soul in
Him was unswervingly united to the God in Him in
that which makes a personality one, namely, Will."[4] As
Lewis understands it, the human will is linked with
the conscious mind of man—that which most obviously distinguishes him from the rest of nature.[5] It is
consciousness that gives man choice—to obey or not
to obey. And it is when man is obedient, when he
wills to unite himself with God, that he finds himself
to be one person—a person whose choices are continually changing him from the very center of his
being into that perfected person that shall be.

For, of course, the personality is *being* perfected.
That man or woman who we really are will come into
its ultimate personhood only in heaven. This is one
reason why, while we are being perfected, obedience
is not an option but an imperative:

Personality is eternal and inviolable. But then, personality is not a datum from which we start. The indi-

vidualism in which we all begin is only a parody or
shadow of it. True personality lies ahead. . . . We are
marble waiting to be shaped, metal waiting to be run
into a mould. . . .[6]

We are God's work of art, and we must suffer ourselves to be moulded. Only with our willing it can He
create in us the person He intends us to be. Paradoxically, it is only as we obey, as we become "slaves to
obedience," that we come into that incredible freedom of the realized and integrated personality. Only
then, by virtue of our being indwelt by God, are we
fully free to collaborate with the Holy Spirit; only then
are we truly creative:

Human will becomes truly creative and truly our own
when it is wholly God's, and this is one of the many
senses in which he that loses his soul shall find it. In all
other acts our will is fed through nature, that is, through
created things other than the self—through the desires
which our physical organism and our heredity supply to
us. When we act from ourselves alone—that is, from God
in ourselves—we are collaborators in, or live instruments
of, creation: and that is why such an act undoes with
"backward mutters of dissevering power" the uncreative
spell which Adam laid upon his species.[7]

The realized and integrated personality, finding its
identity only in God, and no longer seeking it in a role
(wife, mother, father, churchwoman), in a career or
profession (doctor, lawyer, pastor, artist), or in a class
(woman, white-collar worker, black), is no longer
shaped or determined by fears of failure or by what
others think of it. Its justification is in God alone. This
redeemed personality is freed from the superimposi-
tion of the sins, mistakes, and foibles of others and of

those of its own past; it is freed from the rejections it has experienced, both in its past and in its present. It is truly free: free to love—even its own enemies; free to create—in spite of the fears and the hate surrounding it. This personality no longer attempts to relate to others (much less to the Body of Christ) on the basis of expertise of any kind, for it no longer finds its identity in that expertise. Fears, outward pressures, undue domination by others, no longer shape its inner life, nor even—over too long a period—the circumstances of its outer life; secure within its inner being, it is enabled to confront and to deal with these things rather than be shaped by them. It has, insofar as its finiteness permits, *willed* to be one with God. Its will one with its Creator's, it can therefore perfectly collaborate with its Creator. Paradoxically appearing to have lost itself, the personality finds itself for the first time truly creative.

This creativity springs forth from God in us, and, as the New Testament reveals, "originality" is the prerogative of God alone.[8] Man the artist, collaborating with the Holy Spirit, listens to the work; he gets self out of the way and discovers, rather than creates, the work that is waiting to be released from chaos, waiting to be given its form. This listening does not involve only the intuitive part of man. Christ *in* man resurrects the whole of man: his intellectual, his sensory, his emotional, as well as his intuitive being. It is the whole man to whom the living Jesus relates Himself; and it is the whole man who collaborates with Him in the act of creative discovery. This, of course, is what the Great Dance is all about. Committed absolutely to Him, our will becomes one with His. We enter into union and communion with the Source of all creativity, and we find, within ourselves, that we

have become persons. Love flows down from the uncreated into the created, and thence into all other
created beings.[9] To continue to receive of the "bright
metal"[10] being poured into it, each creature must become a channel of this love to others. And it is by
virtue of love flowing through us that we begin to
bless and to name our fellows, calling forth the real
"I," and that we begin to bless and name the beasts,
the plants, and even the inanimate creation.

God's Love in us is the divine energy[11] that overcomes the Fall in each individual life, and it is also the
energy that overcomes the death that intruded into all
of nature. Nature too shall be redeemed. And Lewis
liked to think that God wills to heal nature through
man, by his obedience to find a pathway through
which love can flow to all other creatures. He liked to
imagine that as disobedient man is taken into the
obedient Christ, so is dying nature to be taken into
redeemed man. But, if the mode of nature's redemption can only be speculated upon, the mode of man's
is a certainty: man is to be drawn into that Three-
Personal Life; he is to be pulled into God. "The Christian hypothesis," Lewis writes, "is that God has come
down into the created universe, down to manhood—
and come up again, pulling it up with Him."[12] This is
the message of Love flowing down to us and taking us
up into It. This is the message of the Cross, where the
great reversal of the Fall began. At the Cross Love and
Life were injected into a dying creation and from there
we begin to tread "Adam's dance backwards."[13]

The Great Dance has been from all eternity and first
and foremost in the love that has always been going
on between the Father and the Son. Lewis says,
"What grows out of the joint life of the Father and the
Son is a real Person, is in fact the Third of the three

Persons who are God."[14] To enter into the Dance, then, is to enter the Holy Spirit and to enter the living, dynamic activity of Love that has always been between the Father and the Son.

Obedience is the "holy courtesy" required for entering into the divine relationship. To choose this obedience is, in fact, to choose joy. That is why we first see the joy of obedience in the Godhead. The Trinity is a "co-inherence" in Love:

> [B]eing Christians, we learn from the doctrine of the blessed Trinity that something analogous to "society" exists within the Divine being from all eternity—that God is love, not merely in the sense of being the Platonic form of love, but because, within Him, the concrete reciprocities of love exist before all worlds and are thence derived to the creatures.[15]

But it is in the incarnate Christ that we first see the pattern of perfect obedience. He was, of course, perfect God and perfect Man. But it was as man—in His manhood alone—that He stood, and that He suffered; and it was as man that he learned obedience by the things He suffered.[16] His obedience was perfect. The rhythm and harmony of perfect love undulated through Him even during His agony in Gethsemane and while He was nailed to a cross.[17]

Lewis had a keen sense of the humanity, as well as the divinity, of Christ. This is illustrated quite forcefully in a letter in which he speaks of Christ's human will and feelings:

> God could, had He been pleased, have been incarnate in a man of iron nerves, the Stoic sort who lets no sigh escape him. Of His great humility He chose to be incarnate in a man of delicate sensibilities who wept at the

grave of Lazarus and sweated blood in Gethsemane. Otherwise we should have missed the great lesson that it is by his *will* alone that a man is good or bad, and that *feelings* are not, in themselves, of any importance.[18]

So it is that we see both His "manliness" and His perfect obedience and see more clearly the cost involved in the Gethsemane prayer: "Nevertheless, not as I will, but as thou wilt."[19] A root meaning of the word *obey* is *listen*. To obey is to listen. And Christ listened always to the Father. "I am not alone, the Father is with me. . . . I do exactly what I hear the Father command."[20] It was the Father's will that He, by being obedient unto death, should taste death for all mankind, thereby bringing many sons into glory.[21] By willing always to do the Father's will, Christ became our brother.

Christ practiced, always, the presence of the Father: "Believest thou not that I am in the Father, and the Father in me? The words that I speak unto you I speak not of myself, but the Father that dwelleth in me; he doeth the works."[22] This last note is the key to our own obedience. Not only must we listen in the presence of the Father, but we must let the Son and Holy Spirit respond in obedience through us. Here's where we learn that "obedience and rule are more like a dance than a drill,"[23] and that to listen is the exciting key. He that is at once both further away (Sovereign over all) and closer to us than our breathing (Immanent God) can speak to us. With all our being therefore we must learn to listen to Him. To fail to listen is to lose the harmony of communion with Him Who is Ultimate Reality.

To be obedient is to choose joy, that is, utter reality. And the choosing of joy is, of course, the choosing of

Love Himself. St. John says that loving God and obeying Him is proof that we love our brothers and sisters;[24] and conversely, that loving our brothers and
sisters is proof that we love God.[25] To step outside the
Great Dance is to step outside of Love and back into
the hell of self and separation; it is to step from the
co-inherence of all things, animated by the Love of
God, back into *in*-coherence. We see, therefore, that
love and the choice to obey are inextricably in-
tertwined and related. We choose to love God and
others; or, pridefully, we choose self-love instead.

We are able to step outside the Dance because we've
been given the freedom to do so. We were given a free
will because as mere automata we could never love,
and therefore we could never know infinite happiness.

> If a thing is free to be good it is also free to be bad. And
> free will is what has made evil possible. Why, then, did
> God give them free will? Because free will, though it
> makes evil possible, is also the only thing that makes
> possible any love or goodness or joy worth having. A
> world of automata—of creatures that worked like
> machines—would hardly be worth creating. The happi-
> ness which God designs for His higher creatures is the
> happiness of being freely, voluntarily united to Him and
> to each other in an ecstasy of love and delight compared
> with which the most rapturous love between a man and a
> woman on this earth is mere milk and water. And for that
> they must be free.[26]

This love, of course, is not a feeling: "Christian Love,
either towards God or towards man, is an affair of the
will. If we are trying to do His will we are obeying the
commandment, 'Thou shalt love the Lord thy
God.' "[27]

We know that the incarnate Christ rejoiced always in doing the will of the Father. We know also that we are to imitate Him and that there is nothing in life so important as the learning of this day-by-day and moment-by-moment obedience. We know that it is only when our will is perfectly one with His that we are one with the Divine Trinity's purpose for all creation, or that we know any degree of wholeness and healing. Why then, if all our joy depends upon it, is obedience such a dreadfully hard thing to learn?

This brings us to the very crux of the matter of obedience. Our self-will, swollen with pride, is dreadfully diseased and blemished. It has dark spots in it. It requires a radical conversion. This conversion is painful, for it is the surrender of an inflamed self-will that has been, for years, a usurper; for it to surrender is a kind of death.[28] "The full acting out of self's surrender to God therefore demands pain: this action, to be perfect, must be done from the pure will to obey, in the absence, or in the teeth, of inclination."[29] Obedience, even after a thorough conversion of the will, is an ongoing thing. There is a necessity to die daily to the old self, for "however often we think we have broken the rebellious self we shall still find it alive."[30]

It would be hard to stress too much the unique place of man's will, for it stands, as Lewis says, at the very frontier, that place where man meets God, that place which is "at the mysterious point of junction and separation where absolute being utters derivative being."[31] Here man *wills* to relate to his Creator or, turning to love only the self, *wills* separation:

"There are only two kinds of people in the end: those who say to God, 'Thy will be done,' and those to whom God says, in the end, 'Thy will be done.' All that are in

Hell, choose it. Without that self-choice there could be no Hell. No soul that seriously and constantly desires joy will ever miss it. Those who seek find. To those who knock it is opened."[32]

Lewis says of the damned soul that there is always something it prefers to joy,[33] and that it *wills* to choose it though it gain all the illusions of Hell and lose the utter reality of Heaven.

To enter into a loving, obedient relationship with God is not only to find oneself a child of God, it is also to find oneself, even as the incarnate Lord, a servant to all. Servanthood does not come easily to the proud, that is, to the fallen: " 'Milton was right: . . . The choice of every lost soul can be expressed in the words "Better to reign in Hell than serve in Heaven." ' "[34] On the other hand, even the best Christian, that one who most consistently chooses to serve others, is "not a man who never goes wrong, but a man who is enabled to repent and pick himself up and begin over again after each stumble—because the Christ-life is inside him, repairing him all the time."[35] He therefore differs from others "trying to be good. . . . [T]he Christian thinks any good he does comes from the Christ-life inside him."[36]

The Great Dance is centered in incarnational reality. And obedience, that great theme in Lewis, is the key to joy and harmony with God for all who have been empowered by the Spirit. Man's *will*, on the frontier, chooses either to be indwelt by the real presence of God's Spirit, dying to self-will and self-love; or it chooses to be its own "god." The will can reject Love, and prefer something else to joy. If we reject God, we reject the union that completes us, that brings us into personhood, and that grants access to all true creativity. In rejecting God, we step outside of the Great Dance and into the Bent Will which is ruler of the *in*-coherent planet. " 'There is no way out of the centre,' " Lewis writes, " 'save into the Bent Will which casts itself into the Nowhere.' "[37]

8

THE WAY OF THE CROSS

"In Christ a new kind of man appeared:
and the new kind of life which began in Him
is to be put into us.
How is this to be done? . . .
There are three things that spread the Christ
life to us: baptism, belief, and that
mysterious action which different Christians
call by different names—Holy Communion,
the Mass, the Lord's Supper.
At least, those are the three
ordinary methods. I am not saying there
may not be special cases where it is spread
without one or more of these."
Mere Christianity.

All of man's wisdom, good works, and searching out
are incapable of finding God, as the stories of Orual
and Eustace illustrate (see chapters 5 and 6). Instead,
God and His way of redemption found man. And this
is why the Cross and its *way* of saving man stands at
the heart of the Christian faith, for it is here that the
Life that came into the world in the Incarnation is
poured out for us. Lewis once wrote to his friend Arthur Greeves, "Pagan stories are God expressing Himself through the minds of poets, using such images as

He found there, while Christianity is God expressing Himself through what we call 'real things.' "[1] The "real things" are the actual Incarnation, Crucifixion, and Resurrection of Christ (and our participation in them). Christ's descent into His own creation, His good example, and His teachings were not enough. He had to die and rise again. It is by virtue of what happened in His death that our sins are forgiven, and we receive the Christ-life (the uncreated *Zoe*[2] life as Lewis calls it) into ourselves. At the cross we who believe are initiated into Christ's death and resurrection so that we die to our old sinful natures and are taken into Him. That is why to believe in Christ crucified is God's way of saving us. Some too quickly reject the symbol of the crucifix as a valid symbol for today, forgetting that we must daily take our place in His death as well as in His Resurrection. That is why to believe is to become a Christian.

Satan and the evil spirits hate the Incarnation (and incarnational reality) because in it the God of the Old Testament, He Who is faithful and full of loving-kindness, is made present to our world. In Jesus Christ the full revelation of God is made present to man. This, as John's Gospel shows, is a revelation of light, and to know Jesus is to know the Father and to walk in light. To be in sin is to be in darkness, and to fail to believe in Jesus is to remain in one's sins and in the kingdom of darkness. This believing is manifestly an experiential knowing, a relationship with a Person, as Luther says, closer to us than we are to ourselves.

Believing, therefore, is more than intellectual assent by the conscious mind, for it includes experience of the reality believed in. It is a *knowing* that is experiential, that includes the "deep heart" (the unconscious intuitive faculty), and that results in a new creation.

An idiom the Scriptures employ to denote sexual union expresses the deeper meaning inherent in the word: "And Adam *knew* Eve his wife: and she conceived, and bare Cain."[3] "And [Joseph] *knew* her not till she had brought forth her firstborn son: and he called his name Jesus."[4] We moderns have trouble with the words *knowing* and *believing* for to us these suggest merely intellectual conceptual understanding or assent to propositions without the substantive content of the King James's *to know*.

A believing heart, then, is not one with a mere rational understanding of Christ's being and mission, but is one that has entered into a relationship of trust and love with a Person. Of course, the conceptual belief ought to be there too, but a child or a simple person can be a Christian without understanding what, logically or theologically speaking, a Christian is. We now know that an infant, even as an embryo, can experience rejection by his parents when unwanted and unloved, and can, by the same token, experience their affirmation and love. This receiving, of either rejection or of love, is not on a conceptual level, but is a very real message written into the infant's unconscious mind. Insofar as divine Love is concerned, an infant can *believe*—can, in other words, experientially *know* or receive love—long before he can conceptually comprehend it.

Experiential *knowing* is, in a way beyond our understanding, connected with the blood Christ shed for us. The Old Testament commanded the faithful to abstain from blood "for the life of the flesh is in the blood," and "it is the blood that makes atonement for the soul."[5] Knowing this, our Lord instituted the communion meal after blessing the wine and giving thanks for it: "Drink from it, all of you. For this is my blood, the blood of the covenant, shed for many for the forgiveness of sins."[6] In John, Christ emphasizes the central importance of His blood to regeneration:

> In truth, in very truth I tell you, unless you eat the flesh of the Son of Man and drink his blood you can have no life in you. Whoever eats my flesh and drinks my blood possesses eternal life, and I will raise him up on the last day. My flesh is real food; my blood is real drink. Whoever eats my flesh and drinks my blood dwells continually in me and I dwell in him.[7]

And St. Paul's epistles include frequent reminders of this mystery in reference to salvation, e.g., "through faith in his blood,"[8] justification "by his blood,"[9] redemption "through his blood."[10]

In the work of the Cross there is an ongoing reality, one that must ever be proclaimed in the present tense as well as in its historical past; and that is why Lewis, knowing the human mind can only fully grasp the static, is careful not to speculate too closely on the great mystery of the Cross and of the Atonement. In fact, he is anxious to relieve those whose understanding has been limited or obscured by doctrines that present a static or stunted view of what believing the message or receiving the life of the Cross really is. It is here, at the Cross, that His blood was shed in order that our sins might be remitted. And, in a mysterious way we can never fully understand, as He gave His blood, He gave His Life, and that Life enters into all who truly believe He died for them. This is why to believe in the message of a crucified Christ is God's way of saving us. "We are told that Christ was killed for us, that His death has washed out our sins, and that by dying He disabled death itself. That is the formula. That is Christianity. That is what has to be believed."[11] It is before the Cross, and in no other way, that men are made equal, for the way of the Cross bypasses man's highest wisdom and his greatest and most noble works.

This way of receiving the *Novitas*, the new life, the way of Christ crucified, "is sheer folly to those who are on their way to ruin, but to us who are on the way to salvation it is the power of God."[12] Human wisdom cannot apprehend God; it will always be climbing the stairs of a "new knowledge" (a new *gnosis*[13]) without ever reaching the top; but by the preaching of the Cross God finds man. We cannot by our own efforts climb up to God; instead, He descends to us. That is why it is always safer to dwell on His love for us rather than on our love for Him. What love we have is derivative: what we give to Him in praise, worship, and service, we truly only give *back,* as it comes from Him in the first place.

Reality is, as Lewis says, odd. It is not what one would ever have guessed it to be. And no one ever guessed God's way of redeeming man; in fact, not even His own chosen people, the Jews, had even an inkling of it. A cross was, for them, a symbol of cursedness and the ultimate in abasement. They had a picture in their mind of a Messiah who would not only act in power but who would restore their nation to a position of power, and the awful weakness of one hanging on a cross was, especially in connection with their longed-for Messiah, scandalous beyond words. The Greeks sought a rational God, one whom they could comprehend with their minds. Therefore the idea of a God on a cross was sheerest folly to them. But the very weakness or foolishness of God, as St. Paul says, is stronger than all the wisdom of man. All of man's wisdom and searching proved, and still proves, to be incapable of finding this reality out. Yet, at the proclamation of the message of the Cross, this reality, when believed, is poured into the heart of man.

We have been considering the *believing* that does indeed guarantee salvation in that it is an active reception of Another's Life. Christ in us, the New Man, takes the place of the old man (Adam) or the evil principle in us. We learn to yield always to the presence of this New Man and die daily to the old. We learn to let Him live His life through us, incarnationally, and to collaborate with Him fully, because we discover as soon as we attempt to practice the Christian virtues on our own that we are bound to fail.[14] This believing does not cancel out the moral effort on our part nor the striving to imitate Christ:

> Do not think I am setting up baptism and belief and the Holy Communion as things that will do instead of your own attempts to copy Christ. Your natural life is derived from your parents; that does not mean it will stay there if you do nothing about it. You can lose it by neglect, or you can drive it away by committing suicide. You have to feed it and look after it: but always remember you are not making it, you are only keeping up a life you got from someone else. In the same way a Christian can lose the Christ-life which has been put into him, and he has to make efforts to keep it. But even the best Christian that ever lived is not acting on his own steam—he is only nourishing or protecting a life he could never have acquired by his own efforts.[15]

One of the most unforgettable characters in the Narnia Chronicles is Reepicheep, the Chief Mouse, and "the most valiant of all the Talking Beasts of Narnia."[16] In him is to be seen, among other things, the

reality of the Christian's struggle that always comple-
ments grace. There had been a prophecy said over him
when he was but a baby mouse, and it went like this:

> "Where the waves grow sweet,
> Doubt not, Reepicheep, . . .
> There is the utter East."[17]

The utter East was Aslan's own country, the very end
of the world, and Reepicheep had but one goal and
one aim—to *find* that Land. Whiskers alert and twitch-
ing, sword and buckler ready for battle, long tail wav-
ing about and keeping him in perfect balance, Reepicheep fought, talked, swam and sailed through any
and every barrier that threatened to keep him back
from Aslan's country. On several occasions his quest
nearly cost him his life. Yet he was last seen by Edmund and Lucy to sail his little coracle through the
white lilies in the Last Sea, a sea where the water was
so sweet and so dazzling that it was more like liquid
light; and beyond this silver sea (which was beyond
the sun) towered in plain view the mountains of Aslan's country. His struggle had been long and hard,
but Reepicheep, the valiant one, was almost there.

So we have the paradox: "In one sense, the road
back to God is a road of moral effort, of trying harder
and harder. But in another sense it is not trying that is
ever going to bring us home. All this leads up to the
vital moment at which you turn to God and say, 'You
must do this. I can't.' "[18]

To say this to God is to cease from one's own works
and to allow the indwelling Christ to take over. This
surrender is not an abstract theory but a substantive
reality as the *Zoe* life within us issues forth as supernatural faith, wisdom, knowledge, and agape love: in

other words, as all the fruits and as all the gifts of the Holy Spirit. This incarnational understanding of Christ doing His works through His people should heal the disputes that Christians have often had over "whether what leads the Christian home is good actions, or Faith in Christ."[19] They are but the works of Another. Those acts we do on our own in an unregenerate state have a special purpose Lewis describes in a letter to his friend, Dom Bede Griffiths:

> The bad (material) tree cannot produce good fruit. But oddly, it can produce fruits that by all *external* tests are indistinguishable from the good ones: the act done from one's own separate and unredeemed, tho' "moral" will, *looks* exactly like the act done by Christ in us. And oddly enough it *is* the tree's real duty to go on producing these imitation fruits till it recognizes this futility and despairs and is made a new (spiritual) tree.[20]

Although it is obvious that we must cease from our own works, we can't separate "what exactly God does and what man does when God and man are working together."[21] The Bible, as Lewis says, "puts the two things together into one amazing sentence. The first half is, 'Work out your own salvation with fear and trembling'—which looks as if every thing depended on us and our good actions: but the second half goes on, 'For it is God who worketh in you'—which looks as if God did everything and we nothing."[22] "I and my Father are One,"[23] said Christ, and so too is man one with the Father when Christ and man are in union. This union is the believing that Lewis calls faith in the higher sense.

Besides this higher sense in which Christians understand faith, or the act of believing, there is another, and that too is valid. On this lower level faith simply means the acceptance of Christian doctrines as true; and for a long while Lewis could not understand why this should be regarded as a virtue. After all, one believes the Christian creeds are true, or one does not believe. And certainly one should not in any way work up a subjective state which, if successful, could be described as "faith."[24] Later Lewis understood that this level of belief involved virtue to the extent that it "is the art of holding on to things your reason has once accepted, in spite of your changing moods."[25] It turns out that our emotions and our imagination, our wishes and our desires often "carry out a blitz" on our belief, that is, our conscious, reasoning acceptance, and we must therefore "train the habit of Faith."[26] Once the human mind has accepted a thing as true it does not necessarily or automatically go on regarding it as true. The battle is between faith and reason on the one hand, and avarice, lust, greed, and the like on the other, the imagination and the emotion wavering between the two sides like untrustworthy soldiers.

> Now that I am a Christian I have moods when the whole thing looks very improbable: but when I was an atheist I had moods in which Christianity looked terribly probable. This rebellion of the moods against your real self is going to come anyway. That is why Faith is such a necessary virtue. Unless you tell your moods "where they get off," you can never be either a sound Christian or even a sound atheist, but just a creature dithering to and fro, with its beliefs really dependent on the weather and the state of its digestion.[27]

The way of the Cross stands always against the various ways man devises to earn his own salvation, his own ticket to the Utter East. And on that way we experience the ongoing efficacy of the Cross. We are *being* redeemed, and no static understanding of the reception of the *Novitas* or the Holy Spirit should bar us from continuing to receive. Christ gave us a means by which we can continue to participate in the way of the Cross, by which we continue to receive of His life.[28] St. Paul stresses this teaching of the Master to the Corinthians, who were forgetting, and therefore bypassing, the message of the Cross: "The cup of blessing which we bless, is it not the communion of the body of Christ?"[29] Our Lord had said that "the cup is the new testament in my blood,"[30] but the Corinthians were fast departing from this message and looking to the wisdom of man for salvation. St. Paul has therefore to warn them about their failure to discern the body and the blood in Communion; he has to warn them that to take unworthily of the bread and of the cup is to be guilty of the body and the blood of the Lord.[31]

We see then that Christ has provided in Holy Communion a way for us to continue to participate in His dying and rising again. The efficacy of the Eucharist lies in the fact that it is, in effect, an extension of the ongoing work of the Cross. It is not the only means available to us but it is one commanded by Christ and its efficacy, like that of the Cross itself, bypasses the reasoning mind.

Since we contain this new life in "an earthen vessel," we must continue not only to confess our sins and weaknesses, but to receive of that life through the Lord's Supper. Likewise, just as we continue to participate in Christ's death, dying daily to our old sinful natures, we are also called to participate in His continuing Presence through the indwelling Spirit. His Life is further formed in us by participation in this His resurrection Life. This He poured out on the believers at Pentecost, and this He continues to pour out as vessels are open to receive it. This life is His Spirit. Christ was fully present in His disciples only after He ascended to the Father. This is a great truth of the Ascension. From His seat at the right hand of the Father, His resurrection Life is poured out; it is Christ really present within us, both individually and corporately.

Participating then in the life of the risen Lord makes us an extension of the Incarnation. It is then that we can truly live the life of the servant, for Christ's very power and love flows through us when the channels are cleansed and open. Similarly, this is what "carrying the Cross" means—becoming channels through which His redeeming life can flow. The way of the Cross is ultimately the incarnational pattern of the life of obedience in Christ: "The Father eternally begets the Son and the Holy Ghost proceeds."[32]

From this we see how Lewis perceives the Spirit. Besides being the Spirit of Love that has, from all eternity, been between the Father and the Son, He is the Real Presence of Jesus in the believer. The theme of St. John's Gospel illustrates this: Jesus, once lifted up—in His Crucifixion and Resurrection—communicates the Spirit to man.[33] The Father then continues Jesus' work through those in whom He is formed.

St. Paul determined to "know nothing" among the Greeks and the Hebrews but Jesus Christ and Him crucified. This is the only way man is released from the Law and his own works, is taken into union with Christ, and is given His Spirit. Paul's preaching was empowered, not by human wisdom or eloquent rhetoric, but by a manifestation of the Spirit and power. This is the *way* of the Cross, the way that becomes a channel through which the very life of Christ can flow. By such preaching, true belief is ignited in the spirit of the unbeliever, and, entering into Christ, his spirit leaps alive. This kind of preaching, the kind that literally imparts the Presence, is apostolic preaching. Wherever or whenever this preaching occurs, new churches are born.

In an essay first published in 1946, entitled "The Decline of Religion," Lewis lamented the absence of such preaching. He first affirms the work of the Christian apologists; their work is important, but,

> Their share is a modest one; and it is always possible that nothing—nothing whatever—may come of it. Far higher than they stands that character whom, to the best of my knowledge, the present Christian movement has not yet produced—the *Preacher* in the full sense, the Evangelist, the man on fire, the man who infects. The propagandist, the apologist, only represents John Baptist: the Preacher represents the Lord Himself. He will be sent—or else he will not. But unless he comes we mere Christian intellectuals will not effect very much.[34]

The entire Body of Christ needs the renewal that can come only by and in the Presence of the Holy Spirit. Whether in the preached word or in the sacraments, it is the presence and power of the Spirit that makes the difference. Catholics (and indeed, all Christians) need renewal of the Spirit flowing through their sacraments and their confessional. Protestants (and again, all Christians) need to pray that ancient prayer of the Church, "Come, Holy Spirit, Come," that their preaching might be accompanied by the Presence and power of the Holy Spirit. Then the "infecting," as Lewis calls it, comes.

Herein is the (dreadful to some) exclusiveness of the

Church. There is no possibility for eclecticism in it. In the Presence, unless they *will* to remain separate, men are born anew. Moslems, Hindus, Jews who walk into the presence and power of the Holy Spirit are quickly remade—they become Christians. "By definition," says Charles Williams, "Christendom cannot fundamentally admit the right of an Opposition (to its dogma) to exist; to refuse the Co-inherence [of God and man by His Spirit] is to separate oneself from the very nature of things."[35] To be separate from the Presence is indeed to be separate from all that finally is real. Only through the Church's cry for incarnation, for the presence and power of the Holy Spirit in her midst, can she hope to reach those who are separated from the very nature of things. And in this the *believing* Church is to be at one. Our corporate unity is in the same Spirit that individually indwells us all. This is the co-inherence of Heaven and Earth.

Lewis clearly understood that both the sacraments and preaching are efficacious only as they are "transmitters" of the Life of God—only as they participate fully in the *way* of the Cross, the way God has chosen to redeem man. Because of this knowledge he further understood wherein the true unity of the Body of Christ lies. Never "denominational," he lamented the carnal schisms in what should truly be the "Fellowship of the Holy Spirit" on earth.

Lewis proclaimed the way of the Cross as few others have. Yet he considered himself as called "merely" to create a positive intellectual climate for the Christian faith. When asked if he thought the Spirit was at work in his own writing Lewis replied, "Who am I to say whether Grace works in my own stories? . . . [I]f anything is well done, we must say *Non nobis* [not of myself]."[36] For many, regardless of denomination,

Lewis was a quiet but sure channel of the presence and power of the Holy Spirit. Through him, as through all the preachers who have ever been "sent," belief was sown in the hearts of men.

9

THE WHOLE INTELLECT

*"For what can be known about God is
perfectly plain to them since God himself has
made it plain. Ever since God created the
world his everlasting power and
deity—however invisible—have been there for
the mind to see in the things he has made.
That is why such people are without
excuse: they knew God and yet
refused to honor him as God or to thank him;
instead, they made nonsense out of logic and
their empty minds were darkened."*
Romans 1, Jerusalem Bible.

*" 'It is funny how mortals always picture
us as putting things into their minds:
in reality our best work is done
by keeping things out.' "*
Screwtape, Screwtape Letters.

" 'In our world,' said Eustace, 'a star is a huge ball of
flaming gas.' 'Even in your world, my son,' said the
Old Man, 'that is not what a star is but only what it is
made of.' "[1] This word to Eustace was written many
years after the intellectual blocks to Lewis's understanding of the reality of Christianity had tumbled

down. But long before this time, before he came near to theism or to Christianity, thoughts came to him that would blossom later into his incarnational understanding of all reality.

In 1918, just back from the war, and recovering from wounds in a London hospital, Lewis began reading philosophy as well as writing the poetry that would fill his first book, *Spirits in Bondage*. At this time he began seriously to question certain materialist assumptions. As he looked at a tree, he began to perceive "some indwelling spirit behind the matter of the tree"[2] and he thought that perhaps the primitive idea of a Dryad in a tree was closer to the truth than the modern way of looking at nature. At any rate, he knew that whatever a tree really was, it was certainly more than merely the sum of its parts. It was only a short time after this that he came to believe he too was more than matter, that he was spirit as well as flesh and bone.

The steps Lewis took from here toward his later Christian understanding of nature and man are indeed interesting to trace. From believing rational man to be a pawn in a meaningless and irrational world, he came to understand that rationality itself is a gift from outside the system in which he felt trapped. In fact, man's rationality became the "telltale rift in Nature which shows that there is something beyond or behind her."[3] This outcropping, this incarnation of mind[4] in nature, turned out to be the rock on which the case for naturalism founders; for in assuming the mind to be part of nature and hence irrational, it falls into self-contradiction. As Dr. Kilby has noted: "It is nonsense when one uses the human mind to prove the irrationality of the human mind."[5] But beyond this, he came to understand that the Spirit of God, descending into the heart of man, could not only illumine a faltering and faulty intellect but could put it in touch with divine Reason.

Lewis was a good while in coming to this understanding, partly because his journey into faith was by the road of the intellect. In such a century as ours, he therefore had many intellectual barriers to hurdle. In his own words, "The intellectual life is not the only road to God, nor the safest, but we find it to be a road, and it may be the appointed road for us."[6] Many of us have cause to rejoice that this was the road God appointed him.

Lewis was born November 29, 1898, in Belfast, Ireland, and was sent in 1908, just after the death of his mother, to a boarding school in England. Here the young schoolboy, taken to Church regularly, first heard the Scriptures effectively preached and became himself a Christian. By 1911, however, he had by his own admission "ceased to be a Christian," and by 1913 he was a convinced and outspoken atheist. From this point up to his conversion to theism he rather carefully cultivated his state of intellectual and spiritual unbelief.

In 1924 he had become a lecturer at University College, Oxford, and in 1925 Fellow at Magdalen. His conversion to a belief in God came four years after this, in 1929. But this was a conversion to theism only. Lewis describes his intellectual progression from atheism to Christianity as one from "popular realism" to philosophical idealism; from idealism to pantheism; from pantheism to theism; and from theism to Christianity.[7]

In 1931, three years after his conversion to theism, he explains to Arthur Greeves, his boyhood friend, how he has penetrated the last intellectual barrier to belief. This letter is so remarkable in its recounting of his "grammar of assent" that it is worth quoting at length:

What has been holding me back (at any rate for the last year or so) has not been so much a difficulty in believing as a difficulty in knowing what the doctrine *meant:* you can't believe a thing when you are ignorant *what* the thing is. My puzzle was the whole doctrine of Redemption: in what sense the life and death of Christ "saved" or "opened salvation to" the world. I could see how miraculous salvation might be necessary: one could see from ordinary experience how sin (e.g. the case of a drunkard) could get a man to such a point that he was bound to reach Hell (i.e. complete degradation and misery) in this life unless something quite beyond mere natural help or effort stepped in. And I could well imagine a whole world being in the same state and similarly in need of a miracle. What I couldn't see was how the life and death of Someone Else (whoever he was) 2000 years ago could help us here and now—except in so far as his example helped us. And the example business, tho' true and important, is not Christianity: right in the centre of Christianity, in the Gospels and St. Paul, you keep on getting something quite different and very mysterious, expressed in those phrases I have so often ridiculed ("propitiation"—"sacrifice"—"the blood of the Lamb")—expressions which I c[oul]d only interpret in senses that seemed to me either silly or shocking. Now what Dyson and Tolkien showed me was this: that if I met the idea of sacrifice in a Pagan story I didn't mind it at all: again, that if I met the idea of a god sacrificing himself to himself (cf. the quotation opposite the title page of *Dymer*) I liked it very much and was mysteriously moved by it: again, that the idea of the dying and reviving god (Balder, Adonis, Bacchus) similarly moved me provided I met it anywhere *except* in the Gospels. The reason was that in Pagan stories I was prepared to feel the myth as profound and suggestive of meaning beyond my grasp even tho' I could not say in cold prose "what it meant." Now the story of Christ is simply a true myth: a myth working on us in the same way as the others, but with this tremendous difference that *it really happened:* and one must be content to accept it in the same way, remembering that it is God's myth where the others are men's myths: i.e. the Pagan stories are God expressing Himself through the minds of poets, using such images as He found there, while Christianity is God expressing Himself through what we call "real things." Therefore it is *true*, not in the sense of being a "description" of God (that no finite mind can take in) but in the sense of being the way in which God chooses to (or can) appear to our faculties. The "doctrines" we get *out* of the true myth are of course *less* true: they are translations into our *concepts* and *ideas of that wh*[ich] God has already expressed in a language more adequate, namely the actual incarnation, crucifixion, and resurrection. Does this amount to a be-lief in Christianity? At any rate I am now certain a) That this Christian story is to be approached, in a sense, as I approach the other myths. b) That it is the most impor-tant and full of meaning. I am also *nearly* certain that it really happened.[8]

As Lewis journeyed on into certainty and began to write about it, he was, especially in view of the cur-rent climate of unbelief, mindful of the enormity of the claim he was making. He could never have made it had he not by then safely hurdled certain intellectual barriers and fully satisfied himself that reason, as well as experience, rode with him.

It is mind-boggling to consider that the God who created the billions of suns with their own planets and moons is the same God who called out an Abraham, a Moses, and an Apostle Paul into intimate communion with Himself, the same God whom the prophet Daniel identifies as the Revealer of mysteries to man. This Creator, who causes the stars to move in harmony in their own far-flung galaxies, some as many as 500 million light years away from the planet earth, is the same God who tells a Daniel not only what a pagan king named Nebuchadnezzar had dreamt, but also what the dream means. This interference of Absolute Being in His own creation is what we call miracle, but perhaps from the perspective of most twentieth-century minds, the real miracle consists in the fact that Daniel *believed* and *acted* on his belief. Had he been hampered by the naturalistic view that thought is "essentially a phenomenon of the same sort as his other secretions"[9] he would have had a considerably harder time of it. In fact, Daniel would have been like the king's other advisers: his sages, enchanters, and magicians who said that none could divine the mystery of the king's dream except he be a god—and a god's dwelling was not, they said, with creatures of flesh. And this is what all "misunderstanders" of the Incarnation say: "God is too big, and we are too small: and besides that, He does not dwell with creatures of flesh."

The Incarnation is staggering to the mind. That the Creator of all worlds yearns to be our Father, that He gave Himself to us in such a special way in His Son—the Son whom He sent into our dark world through the womb of Mary, there to grow in the form and flesh of man—that this, the greatest of all myths, happens to be the true one is a thing only to be grasped as the Father Himself gives the power.[10] And we, like Mary, believe in order to receive that "Holy Thing." It is then that we find ourselves to be extensions of the Incarnation by the pouring out of God's Spirit upon us. This too we can only grasp as our Father gives it to us, pouring out upon us our personal Pentecost. Even then it is staggering to the imagination. That the God of all that *is*, not only redeems, but reveals His mysteries and His Presence to mite-sized man, is almost more than the human mind can at first receive.

But Lewis believed it to be true, answering the above objection or "argument from size" with several objections of his own. When he stops to think about it, man knows that size is not of great importance. The brain of one person might be more intriguing than, say, the whole planet Jupiter. Second, size is only relative (especially in an Einsteinian universe). The wheeling galaxies should no more make man feel insignificant than the microcosms of swimming paramecia make him feel significant. Man, small though he is from the crude perspective of measurement, is yet the most complex form in nature. Christian theologians have traditionally considered him the bridge between nature and God, "a little lower than the angels." Not only is he not separated from the numinous, from the Presence of God, he can be— wonder of wonders—a channel of it to the rest of creation.

Yet, though Lewis's path to God was that of the intellect, it should be pointed out in passing that his feelings, heart, and imagination kept pace. Belief in the sense of intellectual assent was accompanied by belief in the second sense as experience of, and trust in, a Person. The steps by which Lewis was "called out" and by which he came to this experiential knowledge are fascinating to the artist, the minister, the scholar, and indeed, to every man in whom there is the capacity for authentic imagination.[11] Lewis's understanding of Joy, of the imagination in its highest, purest state, is central to his epistemology of the Holy

Spirit. Joy for Lewis has to do with the Holy Spirit making God known to an alienated mankind; it has to do with a God Who sends "pictures" to awaken "sweet desire" in pagans, thereby calling them to Himself; it has to do with a God making His Presence known to a humanity fallen from God-consciousness into self-consciousness. His spiritual autobiography, *Surprised by Joy: The Shape of My Early Life,* reveals himself (and man in general) to be separated from the Presence and longing "with lifelong nostalgia" to be united with this Holy Other. *Pilgrim's Regress* might be called an allegorical autobiography of Lewis's estrangement from the Real: it is certainly the tale of modern man's particular plight, of his search for that Something in the universe from which he is estranged.

Man's estrangement from God has always been confused and complicated by his particular intellectual climate and by the characteristic illusions of his era. Lewis wrote to his friend, Dom Bede Griffiths:

> I hope that the great religious revival now going on will not get itself too mixed up with Scholasticism, for I am sure that the revival of the latter, however salutary, must be as temporary as any other movement in philosophy. Of things on the natural level, now one, now another, is the ally or enemy of Faith. The scientists have got us in such a muddle that at present rationalism is on our side, and enthusiasm is our enemy: the opposite was true in the 19th century and will be true again. I mean, we have no abiding city even in philosophy: all passes, except the Word. [12]

But it can perhaps be said that never has an age been more hostile to the Faith than this modern one, nor more completely afflicted with what Lewis calls chronological snobbery—the "uncritical acceptance of the intellectual climate common to our age and the assumption that whatever has gone out of date is on that account discredited."[13] Truth is still truth and error is still error no matter what the date on the calendar is.

> I claim that the positive historical statements made by Christianity have the power, elsewhere found chiefly in formal principles, of receiving, without intrinsic change, the increasing complexity of meaning which increasing knowledge puts into them.[14]

With a passion for honoring truth, Lewis therefore never tires of pointing up the effects of these prejudices on the souls of men. In effect, he takes the blinders off sense-imprisoned men and thereby presents heaven to their sight. For instance, in *Pilgrim's Regress*, the hero's companion John, desiring heaven and that which partakes of the transcendent Good, is taught by philosophy that his finite self cannot enter or know the noumenal world. Yet John, like Lewis himself, succeeds in going where the modern philosopher has said that no man can go. Philosophy has said that those things that the imagination placed as a paradise beyond the world's end were only "in a sense" real, but John ends up seeing—with his own eyes—the Island of his desire. And, what is more, Reason Herself rides with him to the Island and She no longer visits him only by sudden fits and starts. The intellect, in association with the real and the true noumenal (the Holy Spirit), becomes the Holy Intellect, and replaces the glib rationalism of man confined to the world of sense perceptions.

Our period, as Lewis shows, has had no satisfactory

theory of knowledge.[15] That we know reality by God's Spirit within us is an idea simply so foreign to the modern mind-set that even the archetypal memory of it has a hard time emerging in the consciousness of Christian man. That man can know God, the Ultimate Reality, by His Spirit "in-Gracing" him, "by prayer and sacrament, repentance and adoration"—and that this is not fantasy—is a truth lost to modern man, who has (as Lewis once had) an epistemology that accepts as "rock-bottom reality the universe revealed by the senses."[16]

Our educational systems, drawing their theories increasingly from materialist philosophy, have claimed heaven to be off-limits and have taught us to look within ourselves and to this earth for the ultimate good. Worse, they often flatly claim man is only a product of biological, psychological and social forces. There is no "Object," they assume, no objective meaning outside of ourselves and the immediate environment of our senses. Therefore, all the meaning, all the reality we had once attributed to the objective order of the universe, seen and unseen, we attempt to transfer to the "Subject," that is, to ourselves and to our sense-world. Having done this, we find the Subject to be as empty as we have made the Object appear to be:

> At the outset, the universe appears packed with will, intelligence, life and positive qualities; every tree is a nymph and every planet a god. Man himself is akin to the gods. The advance of knowledge gradually empties this rich and genial universe: first of its gods, then of its colours, smells, sounds, and tastes, finally of solidity itself as solidity was originally imagined. As these items are taken from the world, they are transferred to the subjective side of the account: classified as our sensations,

thoughts, images or emotions. The Subject becomes
gorged, inflated, at the expense of the Object. But the
matter does not end there. The same method which has
emptied the world now proceeds to empty ourselves. The
masters of the method soon announce that we were just
as mistaken (and mistaken in much the same way) when
we attributed "souls," or "selves" or "minds" to human
organisms, as when we attributed Dryads to the trees. . .
We, who have personified all other things, turn out to be
ourselves mere personifications. . . . And thus we arrive
at a result uncommonly like zero. While we were reduc-
ing the world to almost nothing we deceived ourselves
with the fancy that all its lost qualities were being kept
safe (if in a somewhat humbled condition) as "things in
our own mind." Apparently we had no mind of the sort
required. The Subject is as empty as the Object. Almost
nobody has been making linguistic mistakes about almost nothing. By and large, this is the only thing that has
ever happened.[17]

Man the subject thus finds himself devastated and utterly without hope in a meaningless cosmos.

Lewis traces this gradual change from medieval to
modern thought in *The Discarded Image* and says, "To
understand this process fully would be to grasp
that great movement of internalisation, and that consequent aggrandisement of man and desiccation of the
outer universe, in which the psychological history of
the West has so largely consisted."[18] This progressive
subjectivization has resulted in an "evil enchantment
of worldliness which has been laid upon us for nearly
a hundred years," silencing the "shy, persistent,
inner voice"[19] within us that cries for heaven—for the
Island of John's desire: "Almost our whole education
has been directed to silencing this shy, persistent,
inner voice; almost all our modern philosophies have

been devised to convince us that the good of man is to be found on this earth."[20]

Physicists, in accepting Dr. Einstein's mathematical description of nature, rejected as inadequate the Newtonian and Darwinian theories that gave rise to the mechanistic and sensate view of man, his mind, and his cosmos; but not before both these theories had profoundly influenced Freud, and through him, the whole of American psychology, the rest of the social sciences, and the humanities. It is strange that the epistemological implications of the new intellectual light, which dawned over four decades ago, have been so very slow to penetrate (when at all) the social sciences and the humanities. Even so, the modern physicists, by their loss of faith in Newton's mechanistic universe, have opened wide a window through which this light can shine. By virtue of this new light and the humility that accompanies it (the loss of certainty that science can explain *what* physical reality is and how *all* things happen), there is power to exorcise at least some of the illusions and barriers which have impeded man's metaphysical desires.

In his book *The Universe and Dr. Einstein*, the physicist-writer, Lincoln Barnett, states that "the materialists are unavoidably faced with the fact that the prime mysteries of nature dwell in those realms farthest removed from sense-imprisoned man," and that by accepting Dr. Einstein's theory, they are forced to abandon their materialistic epistemologies:

> In accepting a mathematical description of nature, physicists have been forced to abandon the ordinary world of our experience, the world of sense perceptions. To understand this retreat it is necessary to step across the thin line that divides physics from metaphysics.[21]

As the materialistic epistemologies are abandoned, however, and as we pass from physics to metaphysics, so to speak, there is a warning that needs serious attention. Lewis warns of a possible junction between two kinds of power, that of the demonic with that of the physical sciences. He foresees a possible return to the *"Anima Mundi* of the magicians" as men attempt to explore the vacuum the faltering materialist epistemologies leave.

In his novel, *That Hideous Strength,* he illustrates what such a return would entail. The scientific organization NICE (National Institute of Co-ordinated Experiments) is not concerned solely with materialistic forms of power. Those in it are also hunting for Merlin's (the magician) power. Ostensibly, their purpose is to promote the power of man over nature, but that purpose has degenerated into a power-struggle between men. As their chief scientist, Filostrato, says, what he and his colleagues are really talking about is "the power of some men over other men with Nature as the instrument. . . . It is not Man who will be omnipotent, it is some one man, some immortal man."[22] In their lust for control of other men and immortality the scientists court the perversely mystical, the dark numinous. "A king cometh," one cries, prepared to be a "channel," for "the Kingdom" coming in "power." And he proves, as do the others in this organization, to be a functioning medium for demonic powers, a vehicle for the power that enslaves other men. The NICE is finally completely controlled by demonic forces. The despair of objective truth, first in a spiritual and moral order to the universe, second, in a material order, has left these men open to the lure of power from any quarter:

The physical sciences, good and innocent in themselves, had already, even in Ransom's own time, begun to be warped, had been subtly manoeuvred in a certain direction. Despair of objective truth had been increasingly insinuated into the scientists; indifference to it, and a concentration upon mere power, had been the result. Babble about the *elan vitale* and flirtations with panpsychism were bidding fair to restore the *Anima Mundi* of the magicians.[23]

Filostrato and the rest who make up the leadership of the NICE no longer believe in a rational universe. All morality is for them "a mere subjective by-product of the physical and economic situations of man."[24] They have lost the Intellectual Good. Reason no longer rides with them. Therefore they would manipulate man even as they have manipulated the rest of nature—and they would do that with the aid of spirits. This is the hideous strength that no merely earthly power is able to withstand. Yet through the hero Ransom heavenly power comes down and overcomes those who have lost the intellectual as well as the spiritual good. The curse of Babel is compounded as it falls on the NICE, for their language is not only changed, it no longer has any meaning: "They that have despised the word of God, from them shall the word of man also be taken away."[25]

In the earlier books of the trilogy, *Out of the Silent Planet* and *Perelandra*, the scientist Weston serves as a frightening example of this junction between materialistic and occult powers. At the beginning of his career as a physicist, Weston has been an out-and-out materialist, and has replaced the hope of immortality with a compelling desire for humanity to "seed itself" from planet to planet, from galaxy to galaxy. The biological survival of human life, no matter what its quality, is all that matters to him in *Out of the Silent Planet.*

When Ransom next meets Weston, on the planet Perelandra (Venus), he is a changed man. No longer a materialist, he has moved his attention from physics to biology, and especially to biological philosophy. He tells Ransom that as a physicist, "Life" had been outside his scope, but now he knows that "All is One." He has become an emergent evolutionist,[26] and his aim is now " 'to spread spirituality, not to spread the human race.' "[27] Now, rather than working for himself, or for science, or for humanity, he works for "Spirit." He has come to a contempt of matter (the one thing he had believed in before), and as an emergent evolutionist he believes the goal of all creation is to become "Spirit." In this view, God is seen as a blind, inarticulate Force.[28] As Weston explains his new religious view of life and his new "mission" to Ransom, likening them to Ransom's "outmoded" Christian beliefs, Ransom cries out, " 'I don't know much about what people call the religious view of life. . . . You see, I'm a Christian. And what we mean by the Holy Ghost is *not* a blind, inarticulate purposiveness.' "[29] To this outburst Weston, in a very superior manner, responds that God is a spirit, and, equating this "Spirit" with mind, freedom, and spontaneity, cries out that we are moving toward "Pure Spirit." When Ransom asks if this spirit is in any sense personal or alive, Weston's face contorts and his voice undergoes a change: " 'Call it a Force. A great, inscrutable Force, pouring up into us from the dark bases of being. A Force that can choose its instruments.' "[30]

Knowing this "Force" experientially, Weston claims ecstatically, " 'I'm being guided. I know now that I am the greatest scientist the world has yet produced. I've been made so for a purpose. It is through me that Spirit itself is at this moment pushing on to its goal.' " To this assertion Ransom replies, " 'One wants to be careful about this sort of thing. There are spirits and spirits you know.' " Finding Weston to equate *the good* with *the spiritual*, Ransom is quick to point out that to be spirit is not necessarily to be good; after all, "The Devil is a spirit," and Christians worship God not because He is Spirit but because He is wise and good.

But Weston, rejecting the idea of a personal God or a Holy Spirit, thinks that spirit itself is the only good and superior to conventional ideas of right and wrong. He cannot, or will not, differentiate between good and evil spirits. Inevitably, he attempts to reconcile good and evil, and tells Ransom, " 'Your Devil and your God are both pictures of the same Force.' "[31] Soon Ransom realizes that Weston not only cannot discern between good and evil powers but is actually possessed by an evil one. The rest of his story is a story of incarnational evil: a supernatural evil force speaking and acting through one who has lost the good of reason and of humanity. Weston has become "the Unman."

In Lewis there is no wedding of good and evil; for him the dark numinous does not partake of Ultimate Reality, of the Uncreated. The pantheist Weston is right in identifying his god or force as within creation itself, for it is finally a created, though supernatural, being. (After all, the Deceiver is, as Lewis says, the opposite of Michael, not of God.) When Weston refers to a Force that pours up into him through the dark bases of his being, he describes very aptly the nature of the demonic as it works against the mind, annihilating the reason and volition, and finally taking over the passive organism that has yielded and opened up to its own Dark Will. It then floods up through the dark passions and instincts, and man is wholly brought into bondage, wholly determined by a force that cannot create but only destroy.

This dark numinous seems to have asserted itself as a "god" in a number of twentieth century writers and thinkers. Insofar as the psychologist Jung attempts to reconcile good and evil the dark numinous is a god in his schema. It is also a god in Freud who, though claiming a wholly biological view of man and mind, came to make of sexuality a phallic god, a "numinosum." Whatever form or disguise it takes, the dark numinous finally is antagonistic to the intellect and to all flesh; it is therefore especially antagonistic to the Incarnation and to man's experiential knowledge of incarnational reality. God, on the other hand, loves man—spirit, soul, and body—and aims to loose him from the darkness and the inessentiality of evil into the radiant substantiveness of the Son of God— the Word, or Reason Incarnate. Satan is the ruler of that world which hates the intellect and the flesh, and the dark spirits, forming a hierarchy under him, make up the "principalities and powers" that plague the fallen planet earth. A juncture of this kind of power with that of the physical sciences would indeed bring all men into bondage. As Lewis shows, it would mean, in the end, the absolute abolition of man.

Meanwhile, the more direct concern we face is the complete secularization of our systems of education, which operate ever more consistently on naturalistic assumptions that would finally reduce the intellect itself to an elaborate computer. In his book, *The Abolition of Man*, Lewis chronicles this *reductio ad absurdum* of the intellect and the consequent drain of meaning and value from his world view as western man has yielded to the spell of materialism. Broadly speaking, until recently there were two different views of man vying one with the other: the Christian and Classical view versus the scientific or biological view. It is the specifically Christian (incarnational) view of man, however, that we are most concerned with here. Suffice it to say that the Classical saw man, through his reason, as a thing above nature and certainly allowed for the supernatural, if it did not always focus on it.

Although the industrial and technological revolutions have lent their momentum to the ongoing alteration in educational philosophy, it is partially through deteriorating and even erroneous ideas of what the term "democratic" means that the supernaturalist view of man is dropping out of education. In societies that separate Church from State, any supernaturalist point of view seems to threaten this division and fall into the category of "religion." Yet, if we define religion as those just principles of belief underlying any world view, we find that the naturalist's assumption—that nature is all there is—involves a commitment of faith equally "religious." It cannot be proven by science any more than the assumption that God exists can. Both are matters of faith.

Yet the loss in our educational system of a transcendent view of man and his cosmos has brought about a crisis in the very spirit of man and is the real basis for the cries of irrelevancy and despair that we hear in connection with higher learning. The humanities, of course, have sustained some of the worst blows from this crisis since their chief value is in the recognition of ultimate essences and the quality of transcendence within the spirit of man.

The problem now confronting higher education is

that of restoring the dimension of transcendence. Traditionally, the central purpose of a college or university has been the preservation, discovery, and transmission of knowledge. As a sanctuary for scholarship, it was to mold "qualified" persons, persons who would be prepared for changes the future would bring. Ethical leadership, respected and trusted, would exercise judgment and govern wisely. Milton describes as generous the education which molds this kind of leader, an education which liberally enlightens the whole man: "A generous education is that which fits a man to perform justly, skillfully, magnanimously all the offices, both private and public, of peace and war."[32] This literary education involved learning the languages of those "industrious after wisdom," and it held a solid recognition of objective and moral values to be attained. T. H. Huxley's words, "A scientific education is as good as a literary," point up the modern contrast to Milton and the traditional understanding of the purposes of education. An exclusively scientific education, materialistic or empirical, by its very nature excludes moral and ethical values and purposes. The present purposes—to produce knowledge, to impart skills, to create "trained intelligence"—though necessary, are materialistic and pragmatic when separated from the greater purpose of imparting ultimate values.

The aims of a college or university are closely tied to its philosophy, and its philosophy is tied, ultimately, to a religious belief or presupposition, whether or not this is understood or acknowledged. Our prevailing naturalistic presuppositions, not to mention the full-blown materialistic philosophies drawn from our scientific methodologies, are apparently considered to be "secular" or "neutral" and therefore, at least in the popular imagination, "democratic." These have erected prejudicial barriers against the supernatural view of man, while at the same time they have re-enforced the naturalistic view.

Contradictory as it may seem, this view may lead to various pantheistic religious views, for naturalism is not necessarily opposed to the notions of an indwelling "god" or cosmic consciousness arising from the biological process.[33] Also, barriers that once held back occult teachings and practices may no longer stand when the biological view of man and mind predominates, because such phenomena are considered to be merely "extra-sensory" and therefore not metaphysical or religious. Actually, pantheistic ideas and practices, as well as those of the occult, have within them the possibility of a real, though destructive, supernatural power, and they have this because man is, in fact, a supernatural being with the capability of opening himself to supernatural powers, both good and evil. These pantheistic and occult teachings, when practiced, constitute a development or opening of the intuitive part of man apart from the safeguard of reason and the power and Presence of the Holy Spirit. Many devotees thus open themselves unwittingly and without fear to forces that can bring them into the bondage of a very real and evil supernatural power. The "god" that naturalism spawns, like that of the character Weston's, is "beyond good and evil" in that it *includes both*.[34] Not only may pantheistic and occult ideologies thus find an entrance into our educational systems under the cover of naturalism, but, due to pressure on those systems to remain "democratic" and "neutral," moral and ethical values go unstated and neglected.

It is a common complaint that the loss of transcendent values has brought about a breakdown of the home, of the church, and of community. Some would see the university as the place where values and transcendent meaning might be restored to society. The fact that the "community of scholars" is now an anachronism belies this arid hope. Scholars themselves complain of how the various disciplines are cut off from each other and share no common values; denying supersensory truth, the best minds cannot agree on any standard of truth. Like many another man, the scholar himself is often resigned to a cosmic relativism while trying to solve his personal problems through a patchwork of psychological theories.

> In the university, the thin smile
> of the intellectual caught in a hell of reflecting mirrors,
> pale cerebrum floating on a spine
> discounting the knowledge of feeling,
> intuition of more than the senses.
> The best, earnest about man's dignity;
> the most, cynical, resigned
> to the mirror for its own sake;
> the worst, positive, infatuated
> with mechanical progress,
> manipulating man by his machines,
> producing ever better means
> to rapidly deteriorating ends.[35]

In a democratic and pluralistic state such as ours there are, of course, diverse ideas of what constitutes truth and reality. Yet today, rather than a political or religious point of view threatening to dominate our system, we are in implicit danger from an unquestioned naturalism. Naturalism, when it ousts the ideologies common to Christianity and to the classical and humanist views of man, becomes itself a dogma and a cult. It becomes *the* religion. In a state where all choices are made "scientifically," that is, by the truth of nature alone, there finally will be no place for democratic disagreement—as B. F. Skinner's *Beyond Freedom and Dignity* forecasts. Even worse, man will perforce be cut off from reason and from spirit, since the transcendent sides of his intellect will not even be recognized. Not to acknowledge the presuppositions or the limitations of science is to raise science to the level of dogma, where it becomes an absolute and is conceived as the only worthy basis of thought and action. In short, it becomes a god.

Herein lies a strange paradox: while the physical sciences themselves are no longer given the uncritical veneration they once commanded, the sensate view of man to which their empirical methodologies gave rise is widely held whether consciously or unconsciously. Though the culture itself is in some ways more pluralistic than ever, its common underlying supposition is a sensate view of truth and reality. This uniformity of ideology has come about largely through the almost exclusively naturalistic education characteristic of the West since the rapid ascension of science in the nineteenth century. Due to our dependence upon "scientific" methodologies for determining truth, we no longer have the diversity that is truly the hallmark of a democratic system of education. "It is not the books written in direct defence of Materialism that makes the modern man a materialist; it is the materialistic assumptions in all the other books."[36]

The critical trend toward a loss of democratic diversity is quite naturally accompanied by other trends toward loss of freedom. As transcendent values are pushed further into the background, we witness the growth of totalitarian ideologies throughout the world. It has often been noted that in our century the intellectual is attracted by one totalitarianism or another. There is even, unbelievably enough, an active hostility to freedom of choice in some quarters. Skinner's book *Beyond Freedom and Dignity* (mentioned above) not only predicts but recommends a future in which choice is nonexistent. From the outset he excludes any moral or ethical system and bases his "utopia" completely on the conditioning and manipulating of man through material reinforcement. As Lewis warns: "I am very doubtful whether history shows us one example of a man who, having stepped outside traditional morality and attained power, has used that power benevolently. I am inclined to think that the Conditioners will hate the conditioned."[37] On the other hand, the nihilist, voting for "nothingness," would bring a sensate age to a quicker end by destroying the culture altogether. Bad as that would be, infinitely worse to contemplate is the establishment of B. F. Skinner's world of behavioral control, for it would constitute a bondage of the very spirit of man.

A similar frightening "solution" to today's problems is reflected in the call for a new system of "scientific" ethics on which to construct a social technocracy. This is the kind of program hailed by the Skinnerians and others. S. E. and Zella Luria, writing in *The Embattled University*, realizing that the educational system cannot be governed when it has lost its yardstick of right and wrong, advocate using the scientific method to come up with a new system of ethics. Social experimentation would decide what is right and wrong. There are other trends toward explaining metaphysical man in just such truncated terms that are equally to be feared. The acceptance of a model of man that is materialistic necessarily undermines ethics based on both the practical reason and on revelation, since they are not quantifiable. Sensate man, faced with a breakdown in his system, is now forced to find an ethic—purely material—made in his own image. Since nature is of itself amoral, it would seem that Dostoyevsky's gloomy prediction has come true: "If God does not exist [i.e., is not believed to exist] *anything* is possible." We may recall the "ethics" created by the Nazis to justify exterminating the Jews.

Traditional man—man spiritual and reasonable as well as physical, man morally and ethically responsible—is the man for whom academic freedom was envisioned. Science, though it never made the claim to be the absolute, has been lifted to the status of dogma. The People, in their gratitude for what technology could do, committed the awful error of making an idol of science. Though no longer bowing down to the scientific method, contemporary man is yet chained to the view of man which arose from its precepts.

Lewis, like his created character Weston, began his adult life as a materialist. Also like him, he discovered materialism to be inadequate. Unlike Weston, however, as his materialism dissolved in the experience of the Living Presence, he found God to be separate from himself, the source of reason, and wholly good. Sending darts of Joy into his closed and alienated mind and world, God was clearly no subjective state of his own mind or body. This Joy proclaimed, " 'I myself am your want of—something other, outside, not you nor any state of you.' "[38] Such is the Object of the holy intellect.

10
THE WHOLE IMAGINATION I: SURPRISED BY JOY

"This [Joy] brought me into the region
of awe, for I thus understood that
in deepest solitude there is a road
right out of the self,
a commerce with something which,
by refusing to identify itself with any object
of the senses, or anything whereof
we have biological or social need,
or anything imagined,
or any state of our own minds,
proclaims itself sheerly objective.
Far more objective than bodies,
for it is not, like them, clothed in our senses;
the naked Other, imageless
(although our imagination salutes it
with a hundred images),
unknown, undefined, desired."
Surprised by Joy.

What is imagination? To most of us it is a vague word. The dictionary defines it as "the action . . . of forming a mental image or concept of what is not present to the senses."[1] Another definition denotes the imaginative faculty itself by which these images or concepts are formed.[2] A third refers to the "power which the mind has of forming concepts beyond those derived from external objects (the 'productive imagination')."[3] This power refers not only to fancy but, more important, to creative or poetic genius, "the power of framing new and striking intellectual conceptions."[4]

Lewis, acknowledging the vagueness of the word, speaks of two ways in which it is often understood, giving examples of both from his childhood. First, "It may mean the world of reverie, daydream, wish-fulfilling fantasy. Of that I knew more than enough. I often pictured myself cutting a fine figure."[5] Second, it is understood in a very different sense that he calls *invention*, and of this he too knew more than enough, for from the age of three he with his brother lived almost entirely in the world of invention. The world they created, replete with chronicles, maps, histories, and water-color-and-ink illustrations, was named Boxen, a land linking their two invented countries Animal Land and "India". The young Lewis's passion for "dressed animals" and "knights in armor" was fully gratified as he invented stories about "chivalrous mice and rabbits who rode out in complete mail to kill not giants but cats."[6] His brother Warren's penchant for steamships, trains, and the land of India was equally gratified as he set about inventing steamship routes to connect the lands. The two together peopled the state of Boxen with such characters as Lord John Big, a frog and prime minister of the land; King Benjamin VII, a bunny; Viscount Puddiphat, an owl and a musician; Rajah Hawki VI, sovereign of India; and many, many more. Fortunately for us, the brothers bound these invented characters and lands into books and illustrations and the record of their inventive genius as children is preserved.[7]

But in neither *reverie* nor *invention* does Lewis locate the truly imaginative experience. About these two experiences he writes:

> In my day dreams I was training myself to be a fool; in mapping and chronicling Animal-Land I was training myself to be a novelist. Note well, a novelist; not a poet. My invented world was full (for me) of interest, bustle, humor, and character; but there was no poetry, even no romance, in it. It was almost astonishingly prosaic. Thus if we use the word imagination in a third sense, and the highest sense of all, this invented world was not imaginative. But certain other experiences were."[8]

There was no Joy—that which leads one into the regions of awe; there was none of the numinous or the transcendent in his wish-fulfilling fantasy or in the world of his invention. But other experiences contained the truly imaginative, those which call for the third and highest definition of the word *imagination:* that of awe at the presence of the Objective Real; that of an intuition of objective truth lying outside ourselves. Joy best describes it.

Joy, on the psychological level, is *sehnsucht:* longing and desire. Two things first taught Lewis this longing: the green Castlereagh Hills that he could see from his nursery window, and a tiny toy garden that his brother made on the lid of a biscuit tin. With these came his first sense of beauty and the longing for the apparently unattainable.

But his first truly imaginative experience, in the fullest sense of awe and of intense desire, also contained Joy as Object. That is, Joy came as a transient Grace, pointing to, and participating in, something totally outside himself and other than he. It was contained in the memory of a memory:

As I stood beside a flowering currant bush on a summer
day there suddenly arose in me without warning, and as
if from a depth not of years but of centuries, the memory
of that earlier morning at the Old House when my
brother had brought his toy garden into the nursery. It is
difficult to find words strong enough for the sensation
which came over me; Milton's "enormous bliss" of Eden
. . . comes somewhere near it. It was a sensation, of
course, of desire; but desire for what? not certainly, for a
biscuit tin filled with moss, nor even (though that came
into it) for my own past. . . . [B]efore I knew what I desired, the desire itself was gone, the whole glimpse
withdrawn, the world turned commonplace again, or
only stirred by a longing for the longing that had just
ceased. It had taken only a moment of time; and in a
certain sense everything else that had ever happened to
me was insignificant in comparison.[9]

His second experience of the truly imaginative came
through Beatrix Potter's *Squirrel Nutkin*, when suddenly he was presented with the "Idea of Autumn"
and this idea pulsed with the transcendent, the
numinous. The third came through poetry. While
reading Longfellow's *Saga of King Olaf*, he came to the
unrhymed translation of *Tegner's Drapa* and the
words,

> I heard a voice that cried,
> Balder the beautiful
> Is dead, is dead . . .

Whereupon the young Lewis was "uplifted into huge
regions of northern sky," and desired "with almost
sickening intensity"[10] that which he could not describe except as something most desirable from which
he was alienated.

That these experiences of longing were an intense desire for heaven, for the Real Presence, was of course something of which the young boy had not the slightest inkling. Later, sharply distinguishing these experiences of Joy from both happiness and pleasure, he said that the quality common to each was that "of an unsatisfied desire which is itself more desirable than any other satisfaction."[11]

The images of Joy were not to be idolatrously mistaken for Joy as Object: that is, the beauty of the flowering currant, the memory of a past memory, or the Idea of Autumn were simply the images through which that Reality could shine, and not the true object of desire. And herein for Lewis is the place of the greatest art. Like the icon it consists of images through which the transcendently real is, as it were, sacramentally channeled. If the image is mistaken for the real, it can no longer be the vehicle through which transcendent truth shines. Instead it becomes "self-conscious" and so a "dumb idol."

Joy, the truly imaginative experience, at its highest level is the *creaturely* experience of "receiving" from the Holy Other. This Joy calls one up out of the mists of self and subjectivity into an objective and suprapersonal Presence. It calls the real "I" forward. Of this Joy Lewis said, "In a sense the central story of my life is about nothing else."[12] Lewis, closed into the world of self, was the "receiver" of that which would never be in his power to control, for "the wind of the Spirit blows where it wills."[13] When Joy darted down into his soul and just as quickly left again, he—after floundering awhile in the bog of introspection—began looking outward in search of the Object whence these experiences came. Lewis was thereby obliged to forsake that alienated status we often prize so highly—

and wretchedly—and come up out of the prison of subjectivity.

There is no doubt that Joy has to do with the work of the Holy Spirit, and that the experience of joy is linked with the word *imagination* in its third and highest sense. But there are several levels even to the truly imaginative, and we must differentiate between that which begins in merely poetic awe and that which includes religious awe. Similarly, we intuit the Real in at least three kinds—the realms of Nature, Supernature, and the Real Presence of God. The awe differs as the *kinds* of reality to be intuited differ, though Absolute Reality, in the Person of the Holy Spirit, can find His way through any one of the three.

It is in the Object, that which invokes the awe, that the difference lies. "The form of the desired is in the desire."[14] When the heavens were opened "in the thirtieth year, in the fourth month, on the fifth day of the month" and the prophet Ezekiel saw "visions of God"[15] he fell upon his face in worshipful awe. In the midst of this he heard a Voice speaking: "And when he spoke to me, the Spirit entered into me and set me upon my feet."[16] Ezekiel was then indwelt by the Object. This is religious awe, and the Object that inspired it was God.

In poetic awe the artist sees, with his newborn intuition, one blade of grass or one dewdrop as it really is. His experience differs from Ezekiel's in that the object giving rise to the awe differs. But the parallels are definitely there. Looking to the object, the artist forgets himself, and in loving that which he sees he becomes totally "absorbed" in it. Possessed by the creative idea, he feels compelled to transpose it into material form. This is poetic awe, capable at any moment of becoming not less, but more, than poetic awe.

It is often with a profound sense of transfigured awe that the artist or the mystic perceives the truths of super-nature or, on a higher level, of God. Then, sometimes flat on his face over what he feels to be his utter inadequacy, he attempts to pass the vision on. Always, too, there is the gap between that which is seen and heard and that which is finally captured—on canvas, in stone, in poetry, in melody. To one who is not an artist or a mystic it seems incredible that Michelangelo felt himself to be a fumbler, and that Isaiah, when he saw the Lord sitting high and lifted up, felt himself to be lost and a man of unclean lips.[17] Even so, it is in humility and awe, and with a plea for incarnation, a plea for enablement to be a servant to the work, that the mystic, priest, or artist *sees* the *Real* and desires to capture at least a gleam of it in his visions and creations, in his relationships with people, and in his worship. To capture this within the mountains, stars and seas, the eternal splendor, rhythm, and melody inherent in the very fabric of the universe; within the individual person, a universe enclosed in human form; within the communion cup, the living body and blood of Christ!—that is his desire.

There is finally a difference in kind between an intuition of the Real Presence and the intuition of a truth in nature or even in super-nature. But the manner in which the revelation comes and the intuitive and experiential nature of the *knowing* is much the same:

The comparison is of course between something of infinite moment and something very small; like comparison between the Sun and the Sun's reflection in a dewdrop. Indeed, in my view, very like it, for I do not think the resemblance between the Christian and the merely imag-

inative experience is accidental. I think that all things, in
their way, reflect heavenly truth, the imagination not
least. "Reflect" is the important word. This lower life of
the imagination is not a beginning of (i.e., not necessarily and by its own nature. God can cause it to be such a
beginning), nor a step toward, the higher life of the
spirit, merely an image. In me, at any rate, it contained
no element either of belief or of ethics; however far pur-
sued, it would never have made me either wiser or better. But it still had, at however many removes, the shape
of the reality it reflected.[18]

In 1954 Lewis was asked to "make a statement"
about his books. In response to this request, he gave
to the Milton Society of America this "guiding thread"
describing the course of the "imaginative man" in
himself.

The imaginative man in me is older, more continuously
operative, and in that sense more basic than either the
religious writer or the critic. It was he who made me first
attempt (with little success) to be a poet. It was he who,
in response to the poetry of others, made me a critic, and
in defense of that response, sometimes a critical con-
troversialist. It was he who after my conversion led me to
embody my religious belief in symbolical or mythopoeic
form, ranging from *Screwtape* to a kind of theologized
science fiction. And it was of course he who has brought
me,in the last few years, to write the series of Narnian
stories for children; not asking what children want and
then endeavoring to adapt myself (this was not needed)
but because the fairy tale was the genre best fitted for
what I wanted to say.[19]

The fact that the "basic man" in Lewis was the imaginative man makes all the more significant what he
says about the temporary cessation of his imaginative

life in the period between childhood and "that wonderful reawakening which comes to most of us when puberty is complete."[20] This boyhood sleep he calls the "dark ages," the period "in which the imagination has slept and the most unideal senses and ambitions have been restlessly, even maniacally, awake."[21] Bereft of the truly imaginative, this stretch of his life dropped a dark curtain over even the memory of authentic joy. Lewis read and loved Arnold's poem, *Sohrab*, during this period but, he notes, "Joy is distinct not only from pleasure in general but even from aesthetic pleasure. It must have the stab, the pang, the inconsolable longing."[22]

At about fourteen years of age,[23] longing and desire instantly returned to him as he glimpsed the words *Siegfried and the Twilight of the Gods* headlined in a literary periodical. What he describes as "pure Northernness" then engulfed him, along with the memory of Joy itself. This Northernness, riding on the wings of Wagnerian music and Norse mythology, was "essentially a desire and implied the absence of its object."[24] It was an imaginative Renaissance of Joy as *longing* that brought with it the gift of an inner awareness of "hungry wastes, starving for Joy."[25] As so often the case with fallen mortals after an awakening from the narcissistic and auto-erotic stages of puberty, Lewis began to experience life as somehow "split." The one part was his secret imaginative life with its search for Joy, and its constant aim to "have it again"; the other—with its school-boy bustle and aims—still clinging to attitudes and lusts ("erotic and ambitious fantasies") gained in the "dark ages."

There are other dangers besides the hazards of adolescence that threaten the life of the true imagination. Even as love differs from lust, so occult experience differs from poetic or religious awe—that is, from the truly imaginative. Lewis warns us of these also—again, from experience. At age ten, he was sent from his father's home in Ireland to study in Hertfordshire (England) where he found life to be harsh indeed. But it was there, living under the tyranny of the impossible headmaster, "Oldie," that he first became what he called "an effective believer."[26] Taken every Sunday to an Anglican Church, young Lewis heard the "doctrines of Christianity . . . taught by men who obviously believed them."[27] He began to read the Bible, to pray, and to attempt obedience; but, as noted before, his habit of introspection caused these practices to be painful ones.

Three years after that, however, his father sent him to a college preparatory school where by his own admission, he "ceased to be a Christian." Having lost his mother to cancer in 1908, and with her "all settled happiness, all that was tranquil and reliable,"[28] he met and felt genuine affection for a motherly house matron who was "foundering in the mazes of Theosophy, Rosicrucianism, Spiritualism; the whole Anglo-American Occultist tradition."[29] Although not intending to destroy his faith, she "loosened the whole framework" of his belief. In exchange for his faith and the onerous false duties of prayer and the religious life, he gained a lust for the occult. "It is a spiritual lust; and like the lust of the body it has the fatal power of making everything else in the world seem uninteresting while it lasts."[30]

The "dark ages" had by then descended upon Lewis, and with it the cessation of authentic Joy. This Joy had been, as well as desire for the apparently unattainable, a *good* and a kind of love.[31] By contrast, his desire for occult experience, rather than love, was a kind of lust. Physical lust for a woman never sees the real woman, knows only its own desire. Even so, a spiritual lust such as this turns inward on itself. Seething with fear, excitement, superstition, and the magician's quest for power, the occult substitutes the way of self and the manipulation by power for the way of love. It is thereby anathema to the true (the self-less) imagination and becomes rather a channel for that which can finally only destroy. Fortunately for Lewis, he soon recognized the quality of illusion and emptiness in all this, but not before his belief in God was further crippled. Hereby released from "the stern truths of the creed" he was soon "altering 'I believe' to 'one does feel.' "[32] Thus, Lewis observed, "From the tyrannous noon of revelation I passed into the cool evening of Higher Thought, where there was nothing to be obeyed, and nothing to be believed except what was either comforting or exciting."[33] As he many years later confessed: "The Enemy did this in me."[34] Lewis had to wait for a renaissance of faith and it eventually came with the return of Joy as Divine Object.

Any descent into the hell of self, by trek through the occult, or by attachment to a particular sin, is harmful to the creative imagination. Because heaven and earth are crammed with living creatures and concrete things, awesome to know in their reality, man is only becoming whole while reaching out to them, i.e., when he is outer-directed. He can only know himself by knowing others, by coming to taste, in a manner of speaking, the incredible variety of *isness* that resides outside himself. Solomon expresses this in part by his proverb: "Iron sharpens iron, and one man sharpens another."[35] So, man is sharpened, Lewis would say, by all that *is* as the eyes of his soul are opened to see and rejoice in it.

It is here that Lewis places the principal value of great art, for by it man is not only brought out of himself but also *revealed* to himself. In this sense, imagination can be a means of grace: Good fiction, by showing us ourselves, can actually produce in us good emotions, good sentiments. But bad fiction and bad uses of the imagination, can serve to aggrandize the self, to lock it up in itself. That is why Lewis found it essential that imagination lead us beyond ourselves to the Source whence we came. And the purpose of the highest art—he says along with Plato and a host of voices not often heard these days—is to do just that. As the Shining One says to the artist newly arrived in heaven:

> When you painted on earth—at least in your earlier days—it was because you caught glimpses of Heaven in the earthly landscape. The success of your painting was that it enabled others to see the glimpses too. But here you are having the thing itself. It is from here that the messages came.[36]

The misuse of the imagination is especially tempting in an anthropocentric age when men's faculties are already directed toward themselves. It is only too easy for a man to identify the power of creating as his own, and himself as the object of all creation, which may lead finally to a radical subjectivism if not solipsism. The danger is analogous to that in an anthropocentric view of religion. Weston, in *Out of the Silent Planet*, was originally a materialist. He, like Freud, held a biological view of man and mind. He was man-centered. Any idea of an objective Divine Being Weston would no doubt have credited to some projection of the human ego onto the cosmos. The changed Weston we find in *Perelandra* has shed his materialism, but rather than now acknowledge an objective and divine reality outside himself, he locates God within himself. He is, even as before his "conversion," totally anthropocentric, but now self-centeredness is nearer to self-worship.

Within any anthropocentric framework, man is tempted to view himself as creator and originator and easily loses the capacity to see himself in the creative process as he really is—a servant out to discover what is already there.[37] Michelangelo viewed the *Moses* and the *David* as already inside the stone, waiting to be freed. As servant to the object, he chipped away the stone, releasing the figures. Modern man can too easily draw a circle about himself, and closed in, discover only a subjective cosmos. With this loss of theocentricity and objectivity, he is necessarily self-centered and becomes "god," as well as creator. Charles Williams's statement about the shift that began with the Renaissance is relevant here: "*Homo* . . . had entered religion. . . . The cry of 'Another is in me' had faded, the Renascence glory was not attributed to the Acts of that Other."[38] The cry of "Another is in me" is thus replaced by "I myself am enough for myself."

The anthropocentric view leads to hubris, to tragic pride; the theocentric view leads to a proper humility and a right interpretation of the *awe* the creature experiences in the presence of the numinous. Concerning this Lewis wrote:

There seems, in fact, to be only two views we can hold about awe. Either it is a mere twist in the human mind, corresponding to nothing objective and serving no biological function, yet showing no tendency to disappear from that mind at its fullest development in poet, philosopher, or saint: or else it is a direct experience of the really supernatural, to which the name Revelation might properly be given.[39]

Lewis's view held that awe presupposes an object (while at the same time, such a view doesn't necessarily ignore the subjective aspect). Objectivity is essential both to Christian theology and mysticism, and to a right understanding of creativity. The anthropocentric view can lead to a quest for greater and greater "originality" and a fragmented subjectivism that approaches complete solipsism.

Originality is, as Lewis has said, the property of God alone. "When we act from . . . God *in* ourselves—we are collaborators in, or live instruments of, creation."[40] Several years ago I heard the distinguished novelist and essayist, Madeleine L'Engle,[41] endorse this incarnational view of creativity. In response to questions from students, she said of herself and of artists in general, "The Spirit comes into us and does it." The artist, she said, is discoverer; he listens to the book that is clamoring to be written; as servant he serves the work. His part is to get rid of self, get self entirely out of the way, so that the work, which has an existence apart from himself, might be released from chaos. He then collaborates, listening always to the work, and gives to it its form, its being. Art is communion, and a writer who so communes, will always write better than he knows. She agreed with Lewis that an author does not necessarily understand his own work better than those who read it. She pointed out that it takes her five to seven years to catch up with the spiritual truth in her own books. Listening to the work, she writes. Her understanding follows. Here she is in accord with the majority of artists who from the Greeks up to our century, generally believed that inspiration came from sources outside and higher than themselves, and that what they presented was more than the subjective excrescense of their own imaginations.

11
THE WHOLE IMAGINATION II: THE TWO MINDS

*"Oh who will . . . make in me a concord of the depth
     and height?
Who make imagination's dim exploring touch
Ever report the same as intellectual sight?"*
                                        "Reason," Poems.

In the preceding chapter we discussed the misuses of the imagination arising from man's pride, his tendency to put himself at the center, rather than finding his true center in God. But equally serious problems arise from our failure to understand and appreciate the ways of *knowing* peculiar to the so-called unconscious mind. This is the intuitive rather than the reasoning faculty, the seat of the creative imagination, the memory, and the gifts of the Holy Spirit. It has much to do with *belief* in the sense of relationship, discussed in chapter 8.

This failure is also rooted in our inheritance of Greek thought, particularly from Aristotle. Aristotle's epistemology confined man's ways of receiving knowledge to the data received through his sense experience and his reason. By synthesizing experience, reason was thought capable of putting man in touch with the real. From these two ways of knowing (experience and reason), both belonging to the conscious mind, he developed his first principles of knowledge. He thus ruled out Plato's third way of knowing, which included the ways of divine inspiration, of the poet and the prophet, of the dream and of the vision, and—most important of all—the way of love. These of course are the ways of the "unconscious" mind: the way of picture, metaphor, symbol, myth, and—with love—the way of Incarnation: that way which brings myth and fact together. Had this way of knowing been retained, we no doubt would not have the somewhat self-contradictory term "unconscious mind" in our vocabulary today, since this way is really not unconscious at all, but involves several different sorts of consciousness.

As the Church, principally through St. Thomas Aquinas, came to accept the Aristotelian epistemology and incorporate it into its theology, the Judeo-Christian understanding of the deep heart (the unconscious mind and its ways of knowing) simply dropped from sight. There were no categories by which to recognize it. Christians and non-Christians alike came to value exclusively the conscious mind and its ways of knowing over those of the unconscious. This has not only greatly hampered the Western Christian's understanding of the creative imagination, but it has mightily suppressed our understanding of the work of the Holy Spirit in man. Indeed, the development and integration of the whole man in his relationship to God, to other men, and to those things within himself have not been fully understood because of our failure to understand our two minds.

Our two minds, so very different, are both vital in

the creative process—one as the matrix of the creative idea and the mythopoeic imagination; the other as the seat of the rational powers which must, after the creative idea is given material form, bring to bear on it a shaping critique. The two minds do not work in ways at all comparable. Intuitive revelations of nature, super-nature, and God are one thing; conscious *thinking about* them is quite another. This discovery, says Lewis, "flashed a new light on my whole life":

> As thinkers we are cut off from what we think about; as tasting, touching, willing, loving, hating, we do not clearly understand. The more lucidly we think, the more we are cut off; the more deeply we enter into reality, the less we can think. You cannot *study* Pleasure in the moment of the nuptial embrace, nor repentance while repenting, nor analyse the nature of humour while roaring with laughter.[1]

Our dilemma, because the conscious intellect is incurably abstract, is "either to taste and not to know or to know and not to taste—or, more strictly, to lack one kind of knowledge because we are in an experience or to lack another kind because we are out of it."[2]

Plain, rational abstractions *about* truth are not truth. Failure to differentiate between the two kinds of knowing can lead to that disease called introspection (a looking inward to find reality), and, because of this, to an art that is "self-conscious." The conscious mind, turned inward on itself, destroys creativity, and ultimately, the good of reason as well, as suggested by the babbling senilities of the aged characters in Samuel Beckett's *End Game*. Finally endless, the introspective abstract analysis of the self becomes a kind of drug to ease the pain of alienation from the *experience* of truth. After a while, the act of hopeless introspection seems to exist for its own sake, exemplified as well in other plays of the Theater of the Absurd.

A. E. Housman has said that anyone can write poetry; only the real poet can rewrite it. The poet sometimes receives his poem very nearly as a whole. Likewise, an entire plot is on occasion *given* to the novelist in a moment of time. The scientist, in a creative flash, sees his "discovery" dancing before his eyes. The creative idea, as Dorothy Sayers points out in *The Mind of the Maker,* contains the whole; the book is there whether it is given form or not, and so with the poem, the sculpture, the painting or the musical motif. Writing about the Creative Idea, she likens it to God the Father—passionless, timeless, beholding the whole work complete at once, the end in the beginning. This, she says, is how we are makers in the Creator's image. It is in the glow of this inspiration that the creative work is set down. Only afterward is the critical, reasoning, conscious mind brought to bear on it, the true rewriting begun. Dorothy Sayers calls the creative energy that molds the creative idea into material form the Son or "the Begotten of that Idea," incarnate in the bonds of matter, working with sweat and passion in time from the beginning to the end. This energy, she says, is the image of the Word. Needless to say, many a poem has been lost, many a plot destroyed because a man, though in the image of God and therefore a maker, has not understood his two minds, their proper work, and their different ways of knowing.

To be introspective is, of course, to have one's eyes off the Object from which the truly imaginative experience comes and on oneself. The conscious mind is, so to speak, looking into the unconscious, and mistaking the track or the sensations which the experi-

ence of Joy leaves in its wake for the experience itself.
When practiced, this introspection can lead to conscious attempts at reproducing within oneself the experience—to try to "have it again." This terrible conscious effort then actually inhibits the unconscious, that very faculty of the mind that would receive the vision of truth.

Had Ezekiel determined consciously to see Yahweh, saying, "I want to have a vision of God," he never would have. Love is the way: love for the Object. This is why, if we seek to be original, we shall never be.[4] If in love for the object, however, we forget ourselves, and look only to the object, there's a possibility that we may become "original" without knowing it. We may, in a manner, become incarnate of the Object; for as we look to the Object, loving it, we participate in its being.

To take a more homely example, let us consider a housewife. One who is outer-directed in the sense that she loves her vases, flowers, rugs, furniture, and is lovingly directed toward them in her work, becomes creative indeed. She may be no artist, but her home will be full of light, beauty and peace. She becomes the creative home maker. Should she suddenly become conscious of herself in her tasks—in other words, be made aware by obligation or misguided ambition that she is to "keep up with the Joneses," that she is to become "original" in her homemaking talents—then her eyes would be off her home and the objects she has lovingly cared for; her eyes would be trained very consciously and analytically on herself. Overly conscious of self as "the creative person," she soon might find that, instead of her running the house, the house was running her—and her family. She would be tyrannized by the house.

Gradually, because of her conscious effort and her lack of a motivating *un*self-conscious love for her home, the fulfilling work that had at one time drawn her out of herself and into creativity would then become a tiring task. Even the vacuuming of a rug can be too much for an overly introspective housewife. She then needs inner healing, a release from the sick self so that she can once again have a healthy and loving interest in her world.

Much of our art is so *conscious* that it tyrannizes us. "All life is worship, all work is worship, all worship is Love," says Rufus Mosely, the great twentieth century Christian mystic. And so it is. Only in loving that which is outside ourselves can we ourselves be whole and free to create. Some misunderstand Dorothy Sayers's emphasis on creative work. She is not saying, "Find your identity in what you do." Rather, she is saying that in knowing yourself as a maker free to function in the image of God, you are actualized—drawn out of the hell of self and into freedom. For us to truly *know* the real, both "minds" need freedom to function and both also need to be trained on the Object. The way of worship and of love is the only way for the artist as well as for the mystic.

Further, it is with our two minds that we, the subject receivers, not only *know*—but are enabled to *believe*. Lewis writes of these two ways of knowing in his poem "Reason." In this poem the Virgin, Athene, personifies reason, a part of our conscious or intelligent, judging mind, and the Mother, Demeter, personifies the imagination, a part of our unconscious mind or deep heart:

Set on the soul's acropolis the reason stands
A virgin, arm'd, commencing with celestial light,

And he who sins against her has defiled his own
Virginity: no cleansing makes his garment white;
So clear is reason. But how dark, imagining,
Warm, dark, obscure and infinite, daughter of Night:
Dark is her brow, the beauty of her eyes with sleep
Is loaded, and her pains are long, and her delight.

Tempt not Athene. Wound not in her fertile pains
Demeter, nor rebel against her mother-right.
Oh who will reconcile in me both maid and mother,
Who make in me a concord of the depth and height?
Who make imagination's dim exploring touch
Ever report the same as intellectual sight?
Then could I truly say, and not deceive,
Then wholly say, that I BELIEVE.[5]

We modern Western men have neglected the Mother
Demeter, and in doing so have defiled also the Virgin
Athene; for it takes both minds working separately yet
in harmony for us to *know*—and, as Lewis concludes
in the poem, to *believe.*

Oh, that the rules and the pictures had never quar-
reled,[6] that reason and the imagination were fully reconciled! John, in *Pilgrim's Regress,* desires the Island
of his vision and he searches for it. A wise old hermit
tells him that the Landlord has sent him the vision, for
He "has circulated other things besides the Rules.
What use are rules to people who cannot read?" But,

The pictures alone are dangerous, and the Rules alone are
dangerous. That is why the best thing of all is to find
Mother Kirk at the very beginning, and to live from in-
fancy with a third thing which is neither the Rules nor
the pictures and which was brought into the country by
the Landlord's Son. That, I say, is the best: never to have
known the quarrel between the Rules and the pictures.
But it rarely happens. The Enemy's agents are

everywhere at work, spreading illiteracy in one district and blinding men to the pictures in another. Even where Mother Kirk is nominally the ruler men can grow old without knowing how to read the Rules. Her empire is always crumbling. But it never quite crumbles: for as often as men become Pagans again, the Landlord again sends them pictures and stirs up sweet desire and so leads them back to Mother Kirk even as he led the actual Pagans long ago. There is, indeed, no other way.[7]

Pictures: metaphor, symbol, myth, dreams and visions; these are the language of the imagination—of the unconscious mind. John in *Pilgrim's Regress* is an allegorical Lewis, for myth led Lewis to reality. His debts to heathenism were, as he said, enormous, for "It was through *almost* believing in the gods that I came to believe in God."[8] "Sometimes I can almost think that I was sent back to the false gods there to acquire some capacity for worship against the day when the true God should recall me to Himself."[9] In this way the young Lewis was drawn out of himself, acknowledged his creatureliness, and learned to worship. True enough, "It is dangerous to welcome Sweet Desire, but," as John finds out, "fatal to reject it."[10] This dimension of awe and of the numinous had been missing from Lewis's childhood religion; that religion had been (like John's) all rules, and so had commanded no imaginative response; its transcendent level had been sheared off. Therefore God had to use "such images as He found in the minds of poets" to arouse the adoration and the worship for that which was outside, and Other than, the young Lewis.

The Muse is a real thing. A faint breath, as Virgil says, reaches even the late generations. Our mythology is based on a solider reality than we dream: but it is also at an almost infinite distance from that base. And when they told him this, Ransom at last understood why mythology was what it was—gleams of celestial strength and beauty falling on a jungle of filth and imbecility.[11]

We see that Lewis never placed reality within art as *image*, or in the imagination as such. On the psychological level, Joy was a desire or intense longing for an Object (Reality) which he could never quite grasp. Joy as Object or Reality itself always eluded him. Reality only darted through the myth: "Joy itself, considered simply as an event in my own mind, turned out to be of no value at all. All the value lay in that of which Joy was the desiring. And that object, quite clearly, was no state of my own mind or body at all."[12] God was indeed the source from which the arrows of Joy shot through the deep heart of Lewis but, in turning to grasp the transcendent, he found only the physical sensations it had left as it winged its way through. Turning inward to find the reality rather than outward, he instantly destroyed the experience by introspection. Then, while listening to music, walking, or reading his poetry, he would attempt to reproduce it:

> He who bends to himself a joy
> Does the winged life destroy;
> But he who kisses the joy as it flies
> Lives in eternity's sunrise.[13]

Turning to the track that Objective Reality leaves in search for the Reality itself is an error that "appears on every level of life and is equally deadly on all."[14] Modern man, imprisoned in his anthropocentric sphere of subjectivity, is especially liable to this error and is especially plagued by the disease of introspection.

Another error lurks in the occasionally capricious

nature of the imagination—of the pictures as they
occur to us. Without the governing influence of Reason and the Holy Spirit, the Muse can mislead. Herein
lies Lewis's controversy with his good friend, Owen
Barfield, an anthroposophist. Barfield's presupposition of the veridical character of imaginative experience was something Lewis could not accept: "The
truth which you attribute to poetic imagination must
be located. . . . Even if poetic imagination has truth, it
vouches only for itself."[15] Lest this argument seem
contradictory to what we've been advancing, we need
to clarify Lewis's position. The veridical character of
either imaginative experience or of the discursive reason is not to be supposed apart from the work and
presence of the Holy Spirit both in the individual and
in the corporate Body of Christ.[16] There are diabolical
as well as divine elements in the art of our myth-
makers and in the dialectic of our finest logicians, because our capacities to reason and to imagine are
fallen. The key, therefore is in the continuing presence
of the Holy Spirit in the midst of God's people. As
John is told in *Pilgrim's Regress*, because both the pictures (the imagination) alone and the rules (law and
rationality) alone are dangerous, the best thing is to
find Mother Kirk, that which the Landlord's Son
brought into the country. Mother Kirk is Lewis's allegorical name for the Church as the Fellowship of the
Holy Spirit, as that mystical body in which man is
both individually and corporately indwelt by the
Spirit of Truth. The Holy Spirit, promised Christ,
"shall lead you into all truth."[17] Both man's reason
and his imagination, apart from the indwelling Spirit,
are lacking in Grace. Both need this infusion of the
Holy Spirit and both need the wisdom and the balance
provided only by the ingifted, indwelt Body Corpo-

rate. Here, in the Fellowship of the Holy Spirit, in light of the Holy Scriptures, are both reason and imagination to be verified.

Another young friend of Lewis's, who was passing through a period of anti-intellectualism, called the knowledge we gain through prayer and love "poetic experience." Replying to this Lewis said: "I do not see what is gained by calling it poetry or 'poetic experience:' for it clearly covers two things *higher* than poetry, and two things different. . . . It is rather that there is a special *un*poetic experience."[18] When this same friend would also make of Christ a poet rather than a philosopher, Lewis responded that in Christ's words, there is to be seen a "keen-eyed peasant shrewdness" fully as much as an "imaginative quality." Lewis thus argued for our accepting every dimension of the reason as well as the imagination, fully recognizing the value of each. The two minds, infused by grace, are to work together as "one man":

Again, if you are suggesting that the Hebrew consciousness was just right and the Greek just wrong, this seems to me to be quite foreign to the tenor of St. Paul's teaching. He seems to hold quite definitely (a) That our Lord has "broken down the middle wall of partition and made one Man," which is quite different from simply bringing errant Hellenism back to Hebraic rectitude, (b) That the "reasonings of the Pagans" (see Romans) are related to the new Faith much as the Jewish Law is. In Galatians he even seems to equate the Pagan bondage to [elemental spirits] with bondage to the Law. . . . That is why I have a great objection to any theory that w[oul]d set parts of us at loggerheads with one another. . . . The Pagans, by their lights may wisely have constructed a hierarchical scheme of Man, Reason ruling Passion politically and soul ruling body despotically. But in Christ there is

neither male nor female, bond nor free. If the whole man
is offered to God, all disputes about the value of this or
that faculty are, as it were, henceforward out of date. You
said in your letter (going further than some w[oul]d go)
that every natural desire per se s[houl]d be regarded as
an attraction of grace. But if so, how much more every
natural faculty.[19]

As already noted, the power to visualize is not to be
mistaken for the true imagination. Lewis has a good deal
to say about mental images, their merits and demerits,
in *Letters to Malcolm*:[20]

The power—indeed, the compulsion—to visualise is not
"imagination" in the higher sense, not the Imagination
which makes a man either a great author or a sensitive
reader. Ridden on a *very* tight reign this visualising power
can sometimes serve true Imagination; very often it merely
gets in the way.[21]

And this is an important point to make. There is a
difference in the power or compulsion to visualize and
the reception of a free and unbidden intuition or revelation. In answer to one young lady's query about his
writing, Lewis provides an example of the latter: "All I
can tell you is that pictures come into my head and I
write stories about them."[22]

That the power to visualize is not *in itself* the imagination is important to keep in mind when considering
the image-making faculty as an "emitter" of man's
"bentness." Much of the contents of the deep heart or
of the unconscious needs healing. Medical missionary
and psychiatrist, Dr. James Stringham, lecturing on
guilt and the need for confession in the healing of the
psyche, speaks of the unconscious mind as the original
computer. If fifty years of one's financial history were

computerized, he says, the one time the person failed
to pay a bill would be the first datum to come up.[23]
And so it is with guilt and experiences of rejection,
as well as diseased or unnatural feelings, in the unconscious. These old unhealed memories come up and are
often accompanied by images or pictures. The unconscious mind banks our emotions, our feelings of
anger, hatred, desire, joy, and love, as well as our
memories. And like the computer, it never forgets the
"unpaid bill," the unforgiven or the unhealed. Desires or thoughts that the conscious mind has repressed are still very active in the subconscious, and
as a further complication, the truly repressed materials
come before the conscious mind only in disguised and
unrecognizable forms. Such images, if confused with
art, can dangerously mislead the artist even as they do
the mental patient.

When in need of psychological healing, psychologist C. G. Jung[24] studied his own images as they came
up from the unconscious. As he recorded these images, he asked himself what he was doing. A voice
within him said, "It is art." Had his conscious mind
agreed, he might easily have fallen into the trap of
identifying the rumblings of an unhealed unconscious
with true art.

Instead he learned how to accept the contents of his
unconscious and how to understand them. He learned
how to behave toward the inner images by isolating
them, personifying them, and thereby gaining objectivity toward them. He later learned to read their
meaning from dreams.

Had he mistaken them for art, he would never have
been able to bring them into the right relationship
with his conscious mind, and thereby understand and
refute them. He would have excluded the conscious

mind's way of knowing and would have lost touch with reality.[25] (This, as Jung well knew, was the philosopher Nietzsche's undoing as well as that of certain poets, writers, and artists.) Such images, objectified and dealt with by the conscious shaping mind, have been used by artists as a key to describing the human mind and heart. But if they are mistaken for oracles or objective truth, independent of the reason and the true imagination, they can lead man into bondage as surely as the graven images of old. It should be said here that what the poets have called "the roving fancy," the seemingly idle and often visual directed and undirected daydream, can play a part in the creative process. Of itself it is not necessarily the distorting record of subconscious difficulties, nor is it by any means the complete imaginative process.

A strongly intuitive approach to art, one that lacks a correspondingly strong logical or philosophical approach, or that fails to understand the Person and work of the Holy Spirit, is dangerous. The reasoning, conscious mind needs to be fully informed and developed in order that the intuitive mind might not be led astray; and both "minds," the soul in other words, must be under the control of and illumined by the indwelling Spirit.

Although Lewis is recognized as one of the most logical minds of this century, he was also an outstanding Christian mystic. Lewis would have flinched at the epithet "mystic" applied to himself, for the term is an unhappy one, having many and varied meanings, one that seldom (it seems) refers to an active Christ-empowered life such as Lewis's. I must therefore quickly qualify what I mean.

That mysticism which seeks, as its goal, union with an abstract deity has no place in Lewis. Georgia Harkness describes the goal of this mysticism as the merger of the finite with the Infinite for a transient but ecstatic period.[26] Two things about mysticism, so defined and practiced, gave him pause:

> 1) That the similarity between Christian and non-Christian mysticism is so strong. I by no means conclude from this that it is un-Christian in the sense of being incompatible with Christianity: but I am inclined to think that it is not *specifically* Christian. . . . 2) I am struck by the absence of such mysticism [so defined] from the New Testament.[27]

Lewis did not believe that we ascend and merge with an abstract God, enjoying a fleeting moment of ecstasy where the soul loses all identity; but rather, that the personal God descends and indwells us, thereby giving us our true identity. His mysticism consists of the knowledge of an indwelling Christ and the practice of the Presence of God within and without. Like the mysticism of Paul and John the Beloved, it is Christocentric:

> Christ be with me, Christ within me,
>   Christ behind me, Christ before me,
> Christ beside me, Christ to win me,
>   Christ to comfort and restore me,
> Christ beneath me, Christ above me,
>   Christ in quiet, Christ in danger,
> Christ in hearts of all that love me,
>   Christ in mouth of friend and stranger.[28]

The pattern of this life is, again, the Perfect Man's. Like Christ, one learns to listen always to the Father and to collaborate with the Holy Spirit. This makes mystics of all those who know the Spirit of God and are indwelt by Him. Christ did His redemptive work exactly as we are to do ours, by "listening." A root meaning of the term *to obey* is *to listen.* He listened always to the Father and always did what He heard the Father say.

This obedient attentiveness is characteristic of the Green Lady in Perelandra who astonishes Ransom by her mystical ways of *knowing.*[29] She has knowledge of other, older worlds and Ransom, in amazement, asks her, "How do you know that?" When she replies, "Maleldil [God] is telling me," he becomes aware of the unseen Presence with them:

> And as she spoke the landscape had become different, though with a difference none of the senses would identify. The light was dim, the air gentle, and all Ransom's body was bathed in bliss, but the garden world where he stood seemed to be packed quite full, and as if an unendurable pressure had been laid upon his shoulders, his legs failed him and he half sank, half fell, into a sitting position.[30]

Maleldil then sends her pictures of Malacandra, a world that Ransom had visited: " 'It all comes into my mind now, . . . I see the big furry creatures, and the white giants. . . .' "[31] After this Ransom, too, learned to hear and to obey. In this way, small and insignificant as he was in the face of seemingly impossible odds, he became the "savior" of Perelandra.

The Scriptures teach that Christ listened to the Father; *trusting* the Holy Spirit, He taught and healed through the power of the Spirit. The apostles learned this from Him.[32] This capacity to collaborate with the Holy Spirit is also given to us.[33] Herein we see the artist and the Christian brought together. The artist, to free the work, must get self out of the way; he must die to self. So it is with the Christian. To do the works that Christ commanded, he must first get self out of the way; he must die to the "old man." And, just as the Spirit gave form and beauty back to the earth which "was without form, and void" when "darkness was upon the face of the deep," so the Christian, listening to God and collaborating with the Holy Spirit, frees the souls of men. Chaotic, fallen, like the earth after the angelic fall, without form and void, the soul cries out to be delivered from chaos, to be given back its form and beauty. The Christian, proclaiming liberty to the soul held captive, calls forth the real person; he frees the prisoner as Michelangelo freed the *Moses*. The true artist and the true Christian collaborate with the Spirit: "The Spirit comes into us and does it."

This is Lewis's mysticism. Perhaps he would prefer the term *supernaturalism*. Incarnational Christianity is supernatural, and Christians are both called and empowered to be extensions of the Incarnation. In this and in this alone—the "mysticism" that acknowledges the Presence of God with us, within us, empowering us—do we find all substitutes for the Real unmasked and stripped away. Lewis not only understood, but experienced, all reality as sacramental, as incarnational—that is as a channel through which God's grace can be known and received. In his Pentecost Sunday sermon, "Transposition,"[34] he suggests the pattern of it. "We catch sight of a new key principle—the power of the Higher, just in so far as it is truly Higher, to come down, the power of the greater to include the less."

To return to where we began, Joy, which first lured Lewis to seek again after God, is in the Christian's life the authentic seal and promise of the Spirit—the evidence, even in times of deep need and sorrow, that we are in communion with Christ, that our Spiritual Marriage with Him is being consummated. Such Joy is the seal of Lewis's mysticism: one that never bypasses the Incarnation, one which recognizes the body, one in which the two minds are given their equally important roles.

Appendix:
THE GREAT DIVORCE

"If you do not take the distinction between
good and bad very seriously, then
it is easy to say that anything you find in
this world is a part of God.
But, of course, if you think some things
really bad, and God really good, then you
cannot talk like that. You must believe that
God is separate from the world
and that some of the things we see in it
are contrary to His will. Confronted with
a cancer or a slum the Pantheist can say,
'If you could only see it from the divine point
of view, you would realise that
this also is God.' The Christian replies,
'Don't talk damned nonsense.' For
Christianity is a fighting religion. It thinks
God made the world—that space and time,
heat and cold, and all the colours and
tastes, and all the animals and vegetables,
are things that God 'made up
out of His head' as a man makes up a story.
But it also thinks that a great many things
have gone wrong with the world
that God made and God insists,
and insists very loudly,
on putting them right again."
Mere Christianity.

To realize the Presence—and potential triumph—of
God in all things, to experience the Incarnation working to redeem the whole of Creation, is to be sensitive
to what St. Paul called "the mystery of iniquity," the
problem of evil. It is to be particularly aware (though
not dismayed by) the evilness of evil and its irreconc-
ilable opposition to good. In response to those who
would try in some way to reconcile good and evil,
Lewis remarked,

> Blake wrote the Marriage of Heaven and Hell. If I have
> written of their Divorce, this is not because I think my-
> self a fit antagonist for so great a genius, nor even be-
> cause I feel at all sure that I know what he meant. But in
> some sense or other the attempt to make that marriage is
> perennial. The attempt is based on the belief that reality
> never presents us with an absolutely unavoidable
> "either-or"; that, granted skill and patience and (above
> all) time enough, some way of embracing both alterna-
> tives can always be found; that mere development or
> adjustment or refinement will somehow turn evil into
> good without our being called on for a final and total
> rejection of anything we should like to retain. This belief
> I take to be a disastrous error.[1]

To recognize that evil in this world is active, powerful, and intelligently malign is not necessarily to question God's final authority nor to deny the unity and
ultimate goodness of what He has created. Rather it is
to recognize that, as St. Paul put it, "Our fight is not
against human foes, but against cosmic powers,
against the authorities and potentates of this dark
world, against the superhuman forces of evil in the
heavens."[2] Believing in Satan or the Devil is not a
requirement for entrance into heaven, but disbeliev-
ing in him will not only blind man to the ravening

Enemy totally committed to devouring—piecemeal if necessary—spirit, soul, and body, but can lead to an image of God that has evil in it. The figure of the Holy Spirit, in those who reconcile good and evil, certainly has darkness in it. And this, as Christ solemnly declares[3] is blasphemous. Such Lewis calls "damned nonsense"—the kind that "is under God's curse, and will (apart from God's grace) lead those who believe it to eternal death."[4]

And there is a very great deal of this nonsense abroad today, even among Christian scholars and theologians. A half century of naturalism's "demythologizing" of the Scriptures along with a concentration on scientific psychology has made it almost impossible for many Christian priests and ministers either to discern the need, or to perform the actions necessary, to release the soul in bondage to both the old fallen self and the Evil One. The individual suffering from depression or oppression, to mention nothing of the one suffering from actual possession, thus remains victimized as he is passed in wearying rounds from minister to medical doctor to psychiatrist to psychologist and back to minister. Also, on the corporate level, Christian fellowships are decimated by their inability to discern or to take authority over the unholy force committed to keeping them back from a shared life of love and power.

On the other hand, there is an equally dangerous error one must avoid:

> There are two equal and opposite errors into which our race can fall about devils. One is to disbelieve in their existence. The other is to believe, and to feel an excessive and unhealthy interest in them. They themselves are equally pleased by both errors, and hail a materialist or a magician with the same delight.[5]

It has been my experience to see not a few souls, once they've repented their blindness concerning the devil's existence and wiles, begin to see him in just about everyone and everything; they begin, in effect, to "practice" his presence. They shortly begin their careers as "exorcists," and turn, in rapid succession, from "exorcist" into "magician." As Lewis points out, the devils who roam this fallen planet in search of souls to devour are delighted with this rapid transformation. Such are the hazards of removing, in this age of naturalism, the "Quality of Disbelief"[6] which has, if not exorcised the devils, at least preserved us from the "superstitions" regarding their existence and from magicians both black and white. In the interest of truth, however, this risk must be taken, for evil can neither be denied nor can it be attributed to God. Possession of the truth about evil and its source is likewise necessary if the Church is to achieve a truly Christian psychology of man and once again assume responsibility for the healing of the oppressed and deluded minds of men.

No modern psychologist or philosopher has understood the unconscious mind and its ways of knowing better than Dr. C. G. Jung. He also knew that there are both diabolical and divine revelations—those that damn, leading to disintegration of the personality, as well as those that inform and lead to "individuation" or "integration" of the personality. Jung himself had from earliest childhood been open to diabolic revelation. It is our misfortune that despite his perception, this great mind reconciled good and evil, made "God, the dark author of all created things . . . alone responsible for the sufferings of the world."[7] He, like the poet, Blake, married heaven and hell, in Jung's words, brought the Above and the Below together. Interestingly enough, also like Blake, he received this reconciliation of good and evil as *revelation*. It led him to say that the psychic life has two poles, good and evil, and that, in a similar fashion, Yahweh and Satan are polar ends of One Being—an argument identical to that Weston presents to Ransom.

When Jung was between the ages of three and four, he had a frightening dream in which he was taken underground and presented to the "Below" god, a horrible enthroned presence in the form of a ritual phallus.

> The phallus of this dream seems to be a subterranean God "not to be named," and such it remained throughout my youth, reappearing whenever anyone spoke too emphatically about Lord Jesus. Lord Jesus never became quite real for me, never quite acceptable, never quite lovable, for again and again I would think of his underground counterpart, a frightful revelation which had been accorded me without my seeking it.[8]

This dream phallus was introduced to him as the "man-eater," a horror that fed on human flesh. Haunted by this image for years, he later recognized it as a ritual phallus. This and several other such dark revelations shaped his life and his thought, and led him to believe and teach that "the dark Lord Jesus," or the dark side of God, and the phallus god are one and the same. Both are potentially destructive. It is interesting to note that the dark force which does in fact so quickly exploit and pervert man's procreative functions, also presents itself as a phallus to be worshipped. In primitive and pagan rites, no less than in present social fact, sexuality is "numinized," enthroned.[9]

From his study of ancient mythology and medieval

alchemy, Jung calls this god the "chthonic" or "underground" spirit and sees it as a *numinosum* (a god) in the life and works of Freud. According to Jung, Freud was "emotionally involved in his sexual theory to an extraordinary degree. When he spoke of it, his tone became urgent, almost anxious, and all signs of his normally critical and skeptical manner vanished. A strange, deeply moved expression came over his face. . . ."[10] Later, Freud said to Jung, " 'Promise me never to abandon the sexual theory. That is the most essential thing of all. You see, we must make a dogma of it, an unshakable bulwark.' "[11] Freud, considering himself completely irreligious, had given up Yahweh, but in Jung's interpretation, he thereby only came into the grip of Yahweh's opposite, the Underground God or chthonic spirit: "Freud never asked himself why he was compelled to talk continually of sex, why this idea had taken such possession of him. . . . I see him as a tragic figure; for he was a great man, and what is more, a man in the grip of his daimon."[12] About sexuality, Jung says that it "is of the greatest importance as the expression of the chthonic spirit. That spirit is the 'other face of God,' the dark side of the God-image."[13]

The dark force has other faces than the sexual one, but Jung notes how very often it wears the sexual mask. His observation explains why, when the intuitive faculty is developed apart from the work of the Holy Spirit, and/or apart from the good of reason, sexuality so often becomes in both art and religion, a *numinosum*. Sexual idolatry of one kind or another then ensues.[14] Whether in art or in religion, the dark force often first fastens on man's procreative functions (whether by fantasy or act) and by this brings him into bondage. The force that can never create but can only destroy would start the process of death in a man at that very point where God intended man to give life.

Because of his theory of good and evil, Jung rejected the Christian revelation of a God Who is only good, and in Whom there is no darkness nor shadow of turning. Even though he never succumbed to materialism, Jung's view of reality ended in anthropocentricity. He came to have what Lewis calls the "inbetween view," that of God as an unconscious Force. While this force is an objective one outside man himself, it also becomes, in Jung's terminology, the unconscious mind. Jung's important concept of Individuation provides that "the unconscious is a process, and that the psyche is transformed or developed by the relationship of the ego to the contents of the unconscious."[15]

At one point, Jung had a momentous experience that made "the cosmic meaning of consciousness . . . overwhelmingly clear,"[16] one that led him to believe his understanding of consciousness was the sole treasure he possessed. He concluded that man, by being conscious, gives to the world its objective existence, becomes "the second creator" of the world: "Human consciousness created objective existence and meaning, and man found his indispensable place in the great process of being."[17, 18] By identifying God as the unconscious force which man's conscious mind must learn to relate to (and to control) Jung finally makes man out to be God.

As we have previously noted, Lewis does not make mind or consciousness an ultimate, but holds always to the Divine Spirit of God, both transcendent and immanent (without and within), as the Ultimate and as man's link with the Ultimate. Consciousness in Lewis's view is nearly a synonym for the rational soul—that which is an incarnation of reason and other spiritual elements in an animal body. But conscious-

ness, however supernatural, is still a created thing—
made in the image of God, but not God Himself. For
Lewis, the Holy Spirit in man, not consciousness, is
the prime treasure man can receive; and by it all his
other gifts, including that of consciousness or rational
soul, are illumined and sanctified.

Those who identify God with some unconscious
force in His creation or with human consciousness
itself are not the only ones to dangerously reconcile
good and evil. Even among Christians there are attempts to explain what Paul was content to leave to
God as "the *mystery* of iniquity." By ignoring this
wisdom, they dangerously blur the distinction between good and evil and hurt our idea of God. To try
to reconcile good and evil from our point of view only
obscures what we already know about the difference
between them and may damage the practice of our
faith.

Charles Williams is an example of a committed
Christian who attempts to reconcile good and evil,
though his approach is quite different from Jung's. To
Williams God is objectively Other, and not to be identified with man or the self; in fact, few have written
better on the hell of self and the wonder of *losing* oneself in Love than has Charles Williams. Jung reconciled good and evil because he believed God was both
good and evil. Insofar as Williams attempts the same,
it is because he believes God to be wholly good and
the *only* supernatural power. Therefore, Evil, though
an active and powerful illusion, to him is finally only
an illusion—only apparent—and a shadow of the
good.

Christian theology has always tried to maintain a
balance here between two equal and opposite errors.
One is the view expressed in the ancient Zoroastrian

faith of Persia, that Good and Evil are two real and equal powers, eternally warring, with neither finally dominant. The second is that since all that is real is good, only goodness really exists, and evil is just one of its masks. This view is common to pantheists, of one sort or another, including various eastern religions.

In between these views, the Christian faith has maintained a third view, known as the Augustinian since Augustine gave it its definitive formulation. Augustine says that God and all God created are totally good. Everything that is, insofar as it *is,* is holy. Even Satan was Lucifer, the Prince of Light, highest of the angels. When Satan turned to evil, he turned to "what was not," to non-being, to nothingness, to nonsense. His bent will could only oppose God by destroying, by striving after nothingness. Likewise, when man chooses evil, he is finally choosing nothingness—that which will only hurt himself and those around him. That is why all who follow the bent will of the Father of Lies will finally wind up the shadowy insubstantial creatures of the dark, as Lewis portrays them in *The Great Divorce.* All hell, the heavenly guide shows the narrator of that book, can finally be contained in a tiny crack between two blades of grass in the soil of heaven. From this classically Christian point of view, Dante and others speculate that a physical hell, insofar as it prevents the damned from disintegrating to complete nothingness, is a severe mercy.

Whatever one's speculations on the final fate of those who refuse to surrender their will to God the Father, it is true that evil bears to good the relationship of the parasite to its host. The very strength that evil has is stolen from things that are good in themselves. One need only think of the metallurgy and logistics that go into a rifle, to see how the bad will of the murderer abuses things good in themselves. Satan as the initiator of evil, along with all evil wills after his, wittingly or unwittingly perverts the good. Most often, man does evil while striving for what Milton called "some fair appearing good"; that is, he does evil to achieve something (like power, or pleasure) in itself good. Nevertheless, his selfish motive and bent act are finally destructive of that good and of himself.

In one sense, evil is finally the highest unreality. But the orthodox view forbids us to see it as a masked form of good—or even willed by God. Evil is willed by the Evil One—by Satan—and by all who choose wrongly. True it is that God will finally thwart all evil purposes and bring good out of them—a good so great we can hardly imagine it. Similarly, the orthodox view sees good and evil (for now) in a real struggle, but evil (or its effects) will one day be entirely abolished. In fact, Christ's triumph on the Cross was the decisive battle in a war that evil is bound to lose.

All of this review of Christianity's historic teaching on evil is necessary to understanding why Charles Williams's view must be criticized. I would hasten to say at the outset that Williams as writer and Christian had a profound insight into faith and practice, and that his works and person have had a great influence for the good on figures as diverse and eminent as T. S. Eliot and C. S. Lewis. Lewis, recommending Williams to a friend, said of him: "His face [while lecturing] becomes almost angelic. Both in public and private he is of nearly all the men I have met the one whose address most overflows with *love*. It is simply irresistible."[19] Williams understood incarnational reality

(Love) and his response to it fired the hearts and imaginations of the great and the small.[20]

Williams was a man who loved greatly and who yearned to see an exchange of love between men—the "old knowledge" of love working. Failing to find much of this, he embarked on a search for a solution that would help him see the apparent evil in the world in a new way. Though his motives were the best, the solution he came to gives rise to a figure of Love and of the Holy Spirit that contains darkness in it.

Because he treasured a vision of the unity of all things, he worked to reconcile not only good and evil, but all opposites. The story of his life, it seems to me, is the story of his untiring genius at work to cause "alien and opposite experiences to co-inhere."[21] There was, he believed, only Love to be known; therefore he synthesized opposites in order to find a "new knowledge" of love that would not only affirm all the universe as good, but also see evil as a mask of that Love.

This, he felt, was precisely the achievement of all the great poets. "In each of them discordant elements are united in one."[22] This is, of course, a truism of literary criticism, but for Williams it means more than esthetic unity; it means a reconciliation of good and evil on a theological level. Evident in his critique of all poets and their poetry is the idea that what the poet needs is the courage to allow the Muse to lead him into the Unity. Those who affirm all images will be led into the knowledge of love. What seems to be missing from this view is the recognition that by itself the imagination can lead into the perverse and destructive as well as into the knowledge of love.

In Williams's mind, Dante was the poet *par excel-*

lence, who had achieved this reconciliation in his *Divine Comedy.*[23] For most readers, Dante's three-part division of the next life reflects the traditional medieval notions of Hell, Purgatory, and Heaven, and the reconciliation would seem to be Williams's rather than Dante's. Yet to understand how Williams reconciles good and evil in Dante, we should examine briefly his view of evil. Like Jung, he thought the notion of the devil was coeval with Christianity. He believed that the Zoroastrian opposition of good to evil, the eternal dualism mentioned above, had tainted early Christian thought. Throughout his works, in order to preserve his vision of the Unity and to show all images as good, he does away with the idea of active powers or supernatural persons electing to do evil in opposition to God. Yet, he retains the mythic and archetypal figures of the demonic. These figures of Satan and his fallen angels only symbolize men who elect "to know good as evil." They have occult powers and demonic gifts, not by an incarnation of an evil spirit or even by collaboration with one, but by a misuse of the one only supernatural power. Abiding in self, they are cut off from the co-inherence; they are therefore *in-*coherent. For Williams's purpose then, Dante's unified system was an ideal symbol. His Satan, forever frozen in the bottom circle of the Inferno, could well be interpreted as the last state of the in-coherent man, rather than as a distinct and operative power.

Hell, in Williams's terminology, is an image of an unchanging state which endures no more *becoming*, and to dwell in the alienated self is to dwell in hell. This insight is of course true, and anyone who has read Williams will be aware of his genius in causing this terrible truth to leap alive.[24] Nevertheless, it is only part of the truth. Surely, for Dante, as for Lewis and the main teaching of the Scriptures and the Church, evil is more than the misuse of the one supernatural power by the individual human soul.

Williams's reconciliation of the good [God] and the evil [Satan] is more clearly seen in his dramas. One can almost say his poetry "led" him to the final figure of Necessity, who represents this reconciliation. Though Williams held the idea of Necessity previous to the dramas, the figure that results seems almost as much a product of his poetry as of his philosophy—almost, at times, a literary invention. The way of the affirmation of all images led him to it.

The figure of Satan first appears in *The Rite of the Passion*, a drama that attempts to show that in some mysterious way good and evil are in relationship to each other—not as opposites, but as substance and shadow. After all, Christ's enemies were the agents used to bring Christ to His fulfillment as Messiah and Redeemer; Gabriel and Satan are not really friend and foe of Christ respectively, but the right and left hand pillars of the way. Love is Christ, who reconciles these opposites. Love says, "Say, what art thou, my angel Satan?" And Satan replies, "Lord, I am thy shadow, only known as hell where any linger from thy sweet accord." Turning to Gabriel, Love says: "What art thou, my angel Gabriel?" And Gabriel answers: "Lord, I am nothing but thy annunciation; thy message and thy summons, and thy call, the Gospel to all men of thy great salvation." Then love concludes: "And I alone am utterly all in all."[25]

The figure of Satan is gradually transformed in the succeeding dramas until it becomes, finally, the Flame representing the Holy Spirit in *The House of the Octopus*. John Heath-Stubbs, writing the introduction to

Collected Plays, a book containing nine of Williams's dramas, states:

> Several interpreters of C. W. (including Mrs. Ridler, Mrs. Hadfield, and Brother George Every) have pointed out that the figure of Satan in this work anticipates a series of figures in the later plays—the Skeleton in *Cranmer,* the Third King in *Seed of Adam,* the Accuser in *Judgement at Chelmsford.* In all these, a figure apparently representing Evil or Death ultimately appears, in the light of eternity, as the instrument of Good. This series really culminates in the Flame in *The House of the Octopus;* but the Flame is explicitly an image of the Holy Spirit guarding over and working in the Church.[26]

This transformation is noted by the commentators. I have yet to see one take exception to it. Neither would I, if this final figure were merely a literary one, symbolizing the power of God to turn even the worst circumstances to the highest good by exorcising and defeating evil. As it is, however, the figure represents Williams's synthesis of good and evil in the unity of all things and purports to be a figure of God.

The Flame, representing the Holy Spirit, is a figure of God that is foreign to me. I can recognize Him even less in the figure that appears in *Terror of Light* explicitly named the Holy Ghost. The Flame and other progressions of this figure, speaking from one mouth both Christ's and Satan's words, hold darkness. Elsewhere Williams takes exception to the figure of God that Milton portrays, because he would not go beyond "dualism"[27] into a synthesizing of the powers. But what about the figure that Charles Williams has come up with? The one that indeed makes this synthesis? As at once the *figura rerum* (the figure of truth) and the figure of Satan, it holds darkness; it is that adverse fate which is "Christ's back." It is the necessity one must choose, in love and with no reservations, as the Will of God. Satan is the other face of Christ.

Perhaps, because of the very image of Him he created, Williams was himself fearful of the Holy Spirit. In his struggle to find "a different kind of solution arising from a new knowledge of the activity of love,"[28] he came up with a Holy Spirit that is not truly the Comforter. Alice Mary Hadfield writes that Williams regarded the compulsion of the Holy Spirit as "horrifyingly disturbing"[29] and immortality as much a threat as a hope. Hints of this are reflected here and there in his writings:

> There are those who find it easy to look forward to immortality and those who do not. I admit that, for myself, I do not. It is true that the gradual stupefaction of the faculties which normally overcomes a man as he grows older seems to make—if not the idea of immortality more attractive—at least the idea of annihilation less so. . . . Whatever else is true, the idea of annihilation is more repellant. But I cannot say I find the idea of immortality, even of a joyous immortality, much more attractive. I admit, of course, that this is a failure of intelligence; if joy is joy, an infinite joy cannot be undesirable. The mere fact that our experience on this earth makes it difficult for us to apprehend a good without a catch in it somewhere, is, by definition, irrelevant. It may, however, make the folly more excusable.[30]

This is so unlike Lewis's "the best wave is yet to come!" Though none looks forward to the process of dying itself, it seems to me that Williams has so firmly convinced himself of the co-inherence of good and evil that he is robbed of joy and the hope of immortality that goes with it.

Charles Williams's affirmation of all images as good led him to an image of God the Holy Spirit which is a frightening one. Nor is this fear the proper awe implied in Lewis's assertion: "Aslan [Christ] is *not* a tame Lion." It would seem that Williams needed deliverance from his own image of God—one that is a mouthpiece for both Christ and Satan—in order to find that the Holy Spirit is in no way an Accuser, that He is a Comforter and not a terror. It has been said that Williams "has shown us how we may best love [in] a fallen world"[31]—by complete acceptance of the world and the affirmation of all images. But if we affirm *all* images, we will also affirm the dark ones, and our final image of God, like Williams's, will of necessity hold darkness.

Williams believed that there is finally no darkness in God, that God is Love, and that this life-giving Love, the primal energy, is only holy and pure. However, by constructing a philosophy that set out to prove evil as only apparent and thus finally identified with good, he ended without the joyous anticipation of immortality and heaven that weaves through all of Lewis's writing.

According to the Scriptures, Satan is the master counterfeiter, the "god" of this world, and the one through whom the diabolical revelations come that plague the mind of man and show up in his myths, his philosophies, his theologies, and his psychologies. Believing in the existence of Satan, writes Lewis, "seems to me to explain a good many facts. It agrees with the plain sense of Scripture, the tradition of Christendom, and the beliefs of most men at most times. And it conflicts with nothing that any of the sciences has shown to be true."[32] He is the Unholy Dark Spirit, the one that aims to bring all creation into bondage, to swallow it up into his darkness and nothingness. It was he who first tempted man to put self first and thereby to commit evil, to want to be God. It is he who demands the unending worship due only to God. By encouraging the reconciling of good and evil, he achieves subtly, and at least partially, this goal.

It is blasphemous to attribute the darkness in Satan, of that arising in any creature, to any Person of the Blessed Trinity. Christ solemnly declared "that any sin of man can be forgiven, even blasphemy against me, but the blasphemy against the Holy Spirit can never be forgiven. It is an eternal sin."[33] Where good and evil are reconciled, the character of the Holy Spirit is presented as at once divine and demonic, and He Who was sent as Comforter, as Stirrer of men's hearts toward God, becomes an ambiguous and fearful figure. This is, even as Jung himself acknowledges, blasphemy.

God's love is eternal; this Love is, in a way past our understanding, Himself. He does not simply *will* our good, He gives Himself entirely *as* our good. "The world is a dance in which good, descending from God, is disturbed by evil arising from the creatures, and the resulting conflict is resolved by God's own assumption of the suffering nature which evil produces."[34] God's Love in us or, we might say, His Holy Spirit within us, is the divine energy that overcomes the evil or darkness in each individual life. Lewis has said, "The union between the Father and the Son is such a live concrete thing that this union itself is also a Person."[35] To blaspheme the Holy Spirit is to blaspheme Love, and God's way of saving man. God is Love, and this Love has been "from all eternity, a love going on between the Father and Son."[36] To fear the Holy Spirit (as many do) is to fear the Love which would re-create fallen creatures. "If you want joy, peace, eternal life, you must get close to, even into the thing that has them. They are not a sort of prize which God could, if He chose, just hand out to anyone. They are a great fountain of energy and beauty springing up at the very centre of reality."[37] To fear and thereby to shun the Holy Spirit is to fear Love and thereby step back into separateness.

The exquisite awe the creature feels in the Presence of the Uncreated is a *kind* of fear:

> O how shall I, whose native sphere
> Is dark, whose mind is dim,
> Before the Ineffable appear,
> And on my naked spirit bear, the uncreated beam?[38]

But this fear is quite different from the horror of the Lord produced in the wicked. Darkness cannot abide absolute Goodness, the Light. This horror consists not in the figure of God, but in the fact that we, as sinners, must die to our old, false, usurping selves, submitting, like Eustace, to Aslan's claws. We are fearful because we know we must have our scaly dragon hides ripped off before we can be thrown into the healing waters and, cleansed, come up into the Presence. Only then are we prepared for that Presence to enter fully into us so that we might cease to do our own works, that Another might take over and love through us.

The attempt to combine good and evil is, I believe, one of the greatest threats facing not only Christendom but all mankind today. The freedom and the welfare of all men is at stake in this issue. The Christian view of the Triune God as well as the Christian view of man are in various ways jeopardized by a powerful intellectual thrust toward this synthesis—one that is, especially as it affects the psychology of man, often subtle and undetected. One of the very few great bulwarks against this ideological thrust that affects us at every level (spiritually, psychologically, intellectually, politically) is the intellect of C. S. Lewis.[39] His books are unique in this century.

God is good. But modern man often seems bent on believing otherwise. His motive for doing so may be reflected in the confession of Orual in *Till We Have Faces:* " 'Do you think the mortals will find you gods easier to bear if you're beautiful? . . . We want to be our own.' "[40] The darkness in the world did not overcome the Light Who came, incarnate, into the world. And it is this Light that enters into all who believe in Him. Of the utter purity of this Light none who know it will question. The whole burden of Lewis's writing, and of this book, is that we must become

> . . . as glass
> To let the white light without flame, the Father pass
> Unstained.[41]

And this is the terror, and this is the glory.

NOTES

Preface

1. C. S. Lewis, *Miracles: A Preliminary Study* (New York: Macmillan Publishing Co., 1977), p. 178.

1. Introduction: Incarnational Reality

1. Clyde S. Kilby, *The Christian World of C. S. Lewis* (Grand Rapids: William B. Eerdmans Publishing Co., 1964), p. 5.
2. Gal. 2:20.
3. Lewis, *Miracles*, p. 177.
4. Ibid, p. 115. See also C. S. Lewis, "Transposition," *The Weight of Glory* (William B. Eerdmans Publishing Co., 1975), *passim*.
5. Lewis, *Miracles*, p. 115.
6. C. S. Lewis, *Surprised by Joy: The Shape of My Early Life* (New York: Harcourt, Brace and World, 1955), p. 221.

2. God, Super-Nature, and Nature

1. Lewis, *Miracles*, p. 93.
2. C. S. Lewis, *Letters to Malcolm: Chiefly on Prayer* (New York: Harcourt, Brace and World, 1963), p. 22.
3. Charles Williams, *The Place of the Lion* (Grand Rapids: William B. Eerdmans Publishing Co., 1969), ch. 2, *passim*.
4. Archetypal images.
5. Angelic hierarchies.
6. Lewis, *Letters to Malcolm*, pp. 21-2.
7. Exod. 33:20, NASB.
8. See 1 Tim. 6:16.
9. Exod. 33:22-3, NASB.
10. C. S. Lewis, *The Silver Chair* (New York: Collier, 1971), p. 215.
11. See C. S. Lewis, *Out of the Silent Planet* (New York: Collier, 1962), pp. 94-5.
12. C. S. Lewis, *God in the Dock: Essays on Theology and Ethics*, ed. Walter Hooper (Grand Rapids: William B. Eerdmans Publishing Co., 1970), p. 35.
13. As also in his fellow Inklings, J. R. R. Tolkien and Charles Williams.

14. C. S. Lewis, *The Screwtape Letters and Screwtape Proposes a Toast* (New York: Macmillan Co., 1962), first Preface.

15. *The Universe and Dr. Einstein* (New York: William Sloan Associates, 1950), p. 14.

16. Ibid., p. 10.

17. Ibid., p. 8.

18. Gal. 2:20.

19. Lewis, *Weight of Glory*, pp. 27-8.

20. Lewis, *Letters to Malcolm*, pp. 122-4.

21. Rom. 8:23, NEB.

22. Rev. 5:13.

23. Rom. 8:21, NEB.

24. Lewis, *God in the Dock*, p. 35.

25. C. S. Lewis, *The Problem of Pain* (New York: Macmillan Co., 1966), p. 150-1.

26. Lewis, *God in the Dock*, p. 46.

27. C. S. Lewis, *The Four Loves* (New York: Harcourt, Brace and Co., 1960), p. 174.

3. Sacrament: Avenue to the Real

1. Lewis, *Letters to Malcolm*, p. 103.

2. 1 Cor. 10:17; 1 Cor. 12:12ff.; Eph. 1:22-3; Col. 1:18, 24.

3. Used in reference to the Church, the adjective *charismatic* refers to the Presence of the Holy Spirit and His gifts, just as *evangelical* refers to the preaching of the Word, and *sacramental* to the ongoing means of grace in worship.

4. It is difficult to find any word or expression that exactly explains the function of the Church's ministry with respect to how the Real Presence of Christ becomes available to His people in the Eucharist. We need to be careful to avoid the errors both of a "magical" understanding of the Real Presence and a "merely symbolic" view. Rather, we need to affirm that the real minister of every sacrament is Christ and that His ministry is accomplished through men of His choosing.

5. In the sense of *anamnesis*, i.e., the bringing forward into the present an event from out of the past, not simply an act of psychological remembrance.

6. Charles Williams's phrase.

7. C. S. Lewis, *Mere Christianity* (New York: Macmillan Co., 1978, p. 65.

8. C. S. Lewis, *Perelandra* (New York: Collier, 1962), pp. 143-4.

9. John A. Mackay, *Christian Reality and Appearance* (Richmond, Va.: John Knox Press, 1969), p. 20.

10. Gen. 3:8.

11. Gen. 4:16.

12. Exod. 33:14, NASB.

13. Exod. 13:21, NEB.

14. Ps. 16:8-9, 11, NEB.

15. Ezek. 38:20.

16. Jon. 1:3, 10.

17. Just as only Moses could enter the Presence of God on Sinai and yet live.

18. Heb. 9:24.

19. From an unpublished letter of C. S. Lewis to Arthur Greeves, June 15, 1930, Wade Collection, Wheaton College, Wheaton, Illinois.

20. Acts 8:14-7; 19:3-6; 10:44-8.

21. Lewis quotes this phrase in the context of arguing against changing liturgical forms simply for the sake of change and thereby hindering the main function of the form, which is to facilitate the *worship* of God: " ' 'Tis mad idolatry that makes the service greater than the god.' " *Letters to Malcolm*, p. 5.

22. 1 Cor. 3:16, NEB.

23. T. G. Jalland, *The Origin and Evolution of the Christian Church* (London: Hutchinson House, 1948), pp. 59-60.

24. Lewis, *Problem of Pain*, pp. 17-25.

25. Lewis, *Weight of Glory*, p. 15.

26. Lewis, *Letters to Malcolm*, p. 102.

27. Ibid., p. 103.

4. Spirit, Soul, and Body

1. C. S. Lewis, *The Great Divorce* (New York: Macmillan Co., 1971), pp. 109-10.

2. Ibid., p. 111.

3. Ibid., p. 107.

4. The faces of the saints have always been noted to shine. Stephen's (the protomartyr) face shone as he was being stoned to death.

5. Although the modern notion of intellect is not identical to that of the Greek *nous*, and the latter term contains meanings not accounted for by the English word, the terms are close enough for our purposes here.

6. Gal. 4:19.

7. For this reason, those who recognize the supernatural have difficulty in communicating with those who recognize only the natural; they literally speak a different language. This is also the reason many Christians have grave difficulty communicating with their own children or with other Christians who, schooled in natu-

ralistic thought, are confused and inexperienced in regard to the Holy Spirit's work in their lives.

8. Lewis, *Miracles*, pp. 175-6.

9. C. S. Lewis, *Christian Reflections* (Grand Rapids: William B. Eerdmans Publishing Co., 1971), p. 65.

10. Ibid.

11. TAO, the Chinese word Lewis uses to stand for "the doctrine of objective value, the belief that certain attitudes are really true, and others really false, to the kind of thing the universe is and the kind of things we are." It is the knowledge of the moral law that is common to all men. Called by others natural law, traditional morality, or the first principles of practical reason. See C. S. Lewis, *The Abolition of Man: Reflections on Education . . . in the Upper Forms of Schools* (New York: Macmillan Co., 1957), p. 12.

12. Lewis, *Miracles*, p. 178.

13. The naturalist believes that the universe simply happened and that our earth and man are what they are by strange or lucky accidents, and this is why "no thorough going Naturalist believes in free will." Lewis, *Miracles*, p. 12.

14. According to naturalists, "Nature might be such as to produce at some stage a great cosmic consciousness, an indwelling 'God' arising from the whole process as mind arises . . . from human organisms." Lewis, *Miracles*, p. 14.

15. Lewis, *Abolition of Man*, pp. 14-5.

16. B. F. Skinner's methodologies predominate in the fields of education and behavioral psychology. The data of the behavioral educationists and psychologists adapts most easily to the data-processing and computing machines that are now entrenched as a basic tool in mass education, testing, and research.

17. Lewis, *Weight of Glory*, p. 27.

18. Lewis, *God in the Dock*, p. 160.

19. Lewis, *Miracles*, p. 115.

20. Lewis, *Problem of Pain*, p. 66.

21. Lewis, *God in the Dock*, pp. 116-7.

5. Till We Have Faces

1. C. S. Lewis, *Till We Have Faces: A Myth Retold* (Grand Rapids: William B. Eerdmans Publishing Co., 1964), p. 226.

2. Ibid., pp. 290-1.

3. Lewis, *Problem of Pain*, p. 48.

4. Ibid., p. 71.

5. Eph. 2:10, JB.

6. Lewis, *Weight of Glory*, p. 10.

7. Lewis, *Great Divorce*, p. 67.

8. Lewis, *Problem of Pain*, p. 63.

6. We've Been "Undragoned"

1. C. S. Lewis, *The Voyage of the* Dawn Treader (New York: Collier, 1971), ch. 7, *passim*.
2. Ibid., p. 75.
3. Ibid., p. 89.
4. Lewis, *Screwtape Letters*, p. xiii.
5. His conversion to Theism had taken place at this point.
6. From an unpublished letter of C. S. Lewis to Arthur Greeves, Jan. 30, 1930, Wade Collection, Wheaton College.
7. Lewis, *Mere Christianity*, p. 95.
8. Lewis, *God in the Dock*, pp. 193-5.
9. Kilby, *Christian World of C. S. Lewis*, p. 187.
10. Lewis, *Christian Reflections*, p. 169.
11. Lewis, *Problem of Pain*, pp. 54-5.
12. I.e., a sentimental view, "determined by feeling rather than by reason." *Oxford English Dictionary*, compact ed., s.v. "sentimental."
13. Lewis, *Letters to Malcolm*, p. 98.
14. Ibid.
15. Ibid.
16. The objective real on the plane of nature, i.e., God, and His grace, joy, peace, etc., as mediated by the Holy Spirit.
17. Lewis, *Surprised by Joy*, p. 168.
18. Twentieth-century man, grievously afflicted with this disease of introspection, is, in an unparalleled way, in the grip of this bondage.
19. Lewis, *Mere Christianity*, p. 87.
20. C. S. Lewis, *Letters of C. S. Lewis*, ed. W. H. Lewis (New York: Harcourt, Brace and World, 1966), p. 155.
21. C. S. Lewis, *Reflections on the Psalms* (New York: Harcourt, Brace and World, 1958), pp. 31-2.
22. C. S. Lewis, *The Pilgrim's Regress: An Allegorical Apology for Christianity, Reason and Romanticism* (Grand Rapids: William B. Eerdmans Publishing Co., 1973), p. 167.
23. Lewis, *God in the Dock*, pp. 123-4.
24. From an unpublished letter of C. S. Lewis to Mr. Karlsen, Oct. 30, 1961, Wade Collection, Wheaton College, Wheaton, Illinois.
25. From the *Book of Common Prayer*.
26. Lewis, *Letters to Malcolm*, pp. 106-7.
27. Lewis, *Letters of Lewis*, p. 232.
28. Lewis, *Problem of Pain*, p. 49.

29. Ibid.

30. Lewis, *Letters to Malcolm*, p. 109.

31. From an unpublished letter of C. S. Lewis to Mr. Karlsen, Oct. 30, 1961, Wade Collection, Wheaton College.

32. Lewis, *Mere Christianity*, p. 142-3.

33. Ibid., p. 168-9.

34. Ibid., p. 169.

35. Lewis, *Problem of Pain*, p. 92.

36. Lewis, *Mere Christianity*, p. 190.

7. The Great Dance

1. Lewis, *Christian Reflections*, p. 169.

2. Lewis, *Letters of Lewis*, p. 141.

3. Lewis, *Christian Reflections*, p. 169.

4. Lewis, *Letters of Lewis*, p. 210.

5. For an explanation of how consciousness in man differs from sentience in the beasts or higher animals, see Lewis, *Problem of Pain*, p. 119-ff.

6. Lewis, *Weight of Glory*, p. 40.

7. Lewis, *Problem of Pain*, p. 90.

8. Lewis, *Christian Reflections*, p. 6.

9. This is, in the works of Charles Williams, the "Divine Co-inherence."

10. Lewis, *Problem of Pain*, p. 139.

11. This is not an abstraction but a concrete reality.

12. Lewis, *God in the Dock*, pp. 159-60.

13. Lewis, *Problem of Pain*, p. 89.

14. Lewis, *Mere Christianity*, p. 152.

15. Lewis, *Problem of Pain*, p. 17.

16. Heb. 5:8.

17. Phil. 2:5-8.

18. Lewis, *Letters of Lewis*, p. 210.

19. Matt. 26:19.

20. Author's paraphrase of John 14:31 and John 5:30.

21. Heb. 2.

22. John 14:10.

23. C. S. Lewis, *That Hideous Strength: A Modern Fairy-Tale for Grown-ups* (New York: Collier, 1962), p. 149.

24. 1 John 5:2.

25. 1 John 3:17.

26. Lewis, *Mere Christianity*, p. 52.

27. Ibid., p. 117.

28. Lewis, *Problem of Pain*, p. 79.

29. Ibid., p. 87.

30. Ibid., p. 80.
31. Lewis, *Letters to Malcolm*, p. 49.
32. Lewis, *Great Divorce*, pp. 72-3.
33. Ibid., p. 69.
34. Ibid.
35. Lewis, *Mere Christianity*, p. 64.
36. Ibid.
37. Lewis, *Perelandra*, p. 216.

8. The Way of the Cross

1. From an unpublished letter of C. S. Lewis to Arthur Greeves, Oct. 18, 1931, Wade Collection, Wheaton College.
2. Lewis, *Mere Christianity*, p. 127.
3. Gen. 4:1.
4. Matt. 1:25.
5. Matt. 26:27-8, NEB.
6. Lev. 17:10-1, repeated in Acts 15:20.
7. John 6:53-7, NEB.
8. Rom. 21:25.
9. Rom. 5:9.
10. Eph. 1:7.
11. Lewis, *Mere Christianity*, p. 58.
12. 1 Cor. 1:18, NEB.
13. *Gnosis* in this context means special esoteric knowledge by which initiates hope to gain salvation.
14. Lewis, *Mere Christianity*, p. 127.
15. Ibid., p. 64.
16. Lewis, *Voyage of the* Dawn Treader, p. 11.
17. Ibid., p. 16.
18. Lewis, *Mere Christianity*, p. 128.
19. Ibid., p. 129.
20. From a letter of C. S. Lewis to Dom Bede Griffiths, O.S.B., Nov. 19, 1950, Wade Collection, Wheaton College.
21. Lewis, *Mere Christianity*, p. 130.
22. Ibid., p. 130.
23. John 10:30.
24. Lewis, *Letters to Malcolm*, p. 60.
25. Lewis, *Mere Christianity*, p. 123.
26. Ibid., pp. 123-4.
27. Ibid.
28. John 6:53-6.
29. 1 Cor. 10:16.
30. 1 Cor. 11:25.
31. 1 Cor. 11:25, 27.

32. Lewis, *Problem of Pain*, p. 139.

33. That this Spirit is the Spirit of Christ is attested to in the Bible (Rom. 8:9-11; Phil. 1:19; Gal. 4:6). And the Spirit, for the Christian as well as for Christ Himself (Rom. 1:4), is the principle of the Resurrection.

34. Lewis, *God in the Dock*, pp. 221-2.

35. Charles Williams, *The Descent of the Dove: A Short History of The Holy Spirit in the Church* (Grand Rapids: William B. Eerdmans Publishing Co., 1968), p. 217.

36. From an unpublished letter of C. S. Lewis to W. L. Kinter, Dec. 23, 1952, Wade Collection, Wheaton College.

9. The Whole Intellect

1. Lewis, *Voyage of the* Dawn Treader, p. 180.

2. From an unpublished letter of C. S. Lewis to Arthur Greeves, ca. 1918, Wade Collection, Wheaton College.

3. Lewis, *Miracles*, p. 29.

4. This mind is not capitalized because "human thought is not God's but God kindled." Lewis, *Miracles*, p. 29.

5. Kilby, *Christian World*, p. 161.

6. Lewis, *Weight of Glory*, p. 50.

7. Lewis, *Pilgrim's Regress*, p. 5.

8. From an unpublished letter of C. S. Lewis to Arthur Greeves, Oct. 18, 1931, Wade Collection, Wheaton College.

9. Lewis, *God in the Dock*, p. 136.

10. "Blessed art thou, Simon Bar-jona: for flesh and blood hath not revealed it unto thee, but my Father which is in heaven." Matt. 16:17.

11. For Lewis the truly authentic imagination is that which contains a sense of the numinous.

12. From an unpublished letter of C. S. Lewis to Dom Bede Griffiths, O.S.B., Jan. 8, 1936, Wade Collection, Wheaton College.

13. Lewis, *Surprised by Joy*, p. 207.

14. Lewis, *God in the Dock*, p. 45.

15. Lewis, *Surprised by Joy*, p. 208.

16. Ibid.

17. From C. S. Lewis's Preface to D. E. Harding, *Hierarchy of Heaven and Earth: A New Diagram of Man in the Universe* (London: Faber and Faber, 1952), pp. 9-10.

18. C. S. Lewis, *The Discarded Image: An Introduction to Medieval and Renaissance Literature* (Cambridge: At the University Press, 1964), p. 42.

19. Lewis, *Weight of Glory*, p. 5.

20. Ibid.

21. Barnett, *Universe and Dr. Einstein*, p. 10.

22. Lewis, *That Hideous Strength*, p. 178.

23. Ibid., p. 203.

24. Ibid.

25. Ibid., p. 351.

26. Lewis calls emergent evolutionism "a third view," one between naturalism (atheism) and supernaturalism (belief in a God outside of nature). He also refers to it as the "Life-Force" view and sees it as a form of pantheism.

27. Lewis, *Perelandra*, p. 91.

28. This theory is not to be confused with the theory of biological evolution. See *Perelandra*, Ch. 7, *passim*, and *Problem of Pain*, *passim*.

29. Lewis, *Perelandra*, p. 91.

30. Ibid., p. 92.

31. Ibid., p. 93.

32. John Milton, "Of Education," in M. H. Abrams et al., *The Norton Anthology of English Literature*, vol. 1 (New York: W. W. Norton and Company, 1962), p. 893.

33. For example, Transcendental Meditation (TM), closely tied to ancient Indian Brahmanism and Hinduism, is a yoga technique used to bring one into union with "Ultimate Reality." Claiming that TM is "nothing more than a simple mechanical technique," the International Meditation Society (IMS) which is the parent organization has persuaded the U. S. Dept. of Health, Education and Welfare to donate over $50,000 for the training of public school teachers so that they may in turn train their students in TM. The Illinois and Connecticut legislatures have passed resolutions encouraging the teaching of TM; other states are considering similar resolutions.

34. A view of God that would reconcile good and evil (making Satan the "back" of Christ, or the polar end of a god who is at once good and evil) is common to the works of the poet Blake, the philosopher Nietzsche, and the psychologist Jung.

35. Robert Siegel, from an unpublished manuscript, copyright © Robert Siegel, 1977.

36. Lewis, *God in the Dock*, p. 93.

37. Lewis, *Abolition of Man*, p. 78.

38. Lewis, *Surprised by Joy*, p. 221.

10. The Whole Imagination I: Surprised by Joy

1. *The Oxford English Dictionary*, compact ed., s.v. "imagination."

2. Ibid.

3. Ibid.

4. Ibid.

5. Lewis, *Surprised by Joy*, p. 15.

6. Ibid., p. 13.

7. In the Wade Collection, Wheaton College.

8. Lewis, *Surprised by Joy*, pp. 15-6.

9. Ibid.

10. Ibid., p. 17.

11. Ibid., p. 17-8.

12. Ibid., p. 17.

13. John 3:8.

14. Lewis, *Surprised by Joy*, p. 220.

15. Ezek. 1:1.

16. Ezek. 2:2.

17. Isa. 6:5.

18. Lewis, *Surprised by Joy*, p. 167.

19. Lewis, *Letters of Lewis*, p. 260.

20. Lewis, *Surprised by Joy*, p. 71.

21. Ibid.

22. Ibid., p. 72.

23. Between 1911-13, when Lewis was a student at Cherbourg House ("Chartres"), a prep school in Malvern.

24. Lewis, *Surprised by Joy*, p. 82.

25. Ibid., p. 78.

26. Ibid., p. 33.

27. Ibid.

28. Ibid., p. 21.

29. Ibid., p. 59.

30. Ibid., p. 60.

31. Ibid., p. 220.

32. Ibid., p. 60.

33. Ibid.

34. Ibid.

35. Prov. 27:17.

36. Lewis, *Great Divorce*, p. 80.

37. Dorothy Sayers's comparison of divine and human creativity, *The Mind of the Maker*, recently reissued (San Francisco: Harper and Row, 1979), is the classic statement on this theme.

38. Williams, *The Descent of the Dove*, p. 161.

39. Lewis, *Problem of Pain*, p. 20.

40. Ibid., p. 102.

41. Madeleine L'Engle, Newberry Award winner with her book, *A Wrinkle in Time*, has written some of her ideas on creativity in *A Circle of Quiet*. The above remarks were taken from classroom discussions she led at Wheaton College in 1974.

11. The Whole Imagination II: The Two Minds

1. Lewis, *God in the Dock,* pp. 65-6.
2. Ibid., p. 65.
3. See Sayers, *Mind of the Maker,* especially chs. 2-4.
4. Lewis's first attempt at poetry—after the "dark ages" of his adolescence had passed and Joy had returned riding on the wings of "Northernness"—fell to pieces under the weight of his attempted "originality." See Lewis, *Surprised by Joy,* p. 74.
5. C. S. Lewis, *Poems,* ed. Walter Hooper (New York: Harcourt, Brace and World, 1964), p. 81.
6. The rules—the language of the conscious mind (law and rationality); the pictures—the language of the unconscious mind (imagination).
7. Lewis, *Pilgrim's Regress,* pp. 152-3.
8. From an unpublished letter of C. S. Lewis to Sr. Penelope, C.S.M.V., July 9, 1939, Wade Collection, Wheaton College.
9. Lewis, *Surprised by Joy,* p. 77.
10. Lewis, *Pilgrim's Regress,* p. 156.
11. Lewis, *Perelandra,* p. 201.
12. Lewis, *Surprised by Joy,* p. 220.
13. "Eternity," by William Blake.
14. Lewis, *Surprised by Joy,* p. 168.
15. "The Great War" correspondence between Lewis and Owen Barfield, Wade Collection, Wheaton College.
16. The Scriptural revelation of Jesus, the Divine Word, can degenerate into Law. The Church as a mere body of men holding the same precepts is not Mother Kirk, but the Church as the Fellowship of the Holy Spirit is.
17. John 16:13.
18. From an unpublished letter of C. S. Lewis to Dom Bede Griffiths, O.S.B., undated (ca. July-Sept. 1936), Wade Collection, Wheaton College.
19. From an unpublished letter of C. S. Lewis to Dom Bede Griffiths, O.S.B., May 23, 1936, Wade Collection, Wheaton College.
20. See chs. 16-8.
21. Ibid., p. 85.
22. From an unpublished letter of C. S. Lewis to Susan Salzbert, Feb. 5, 1960, Wade Collection, Wheaton College.
23. Dr. Stringham helped set up the first psychiatric clinic in India and is a leader in the Schools of Pastoral Care.
24. It is not to be thought that in using the example of Jung we are fully endorsing either the overall direction of his thinking or his specific ideas about the relationship between the conscious

and unconscious minds. Jung's thought presents many problems for the Christian, not the least being the conception of good and evil as two poles of one Force, or two sides of one "god" (see Appendix for a discussion of Jung's views about good and evil). Nevertheless, Jung had a profound understanding of the two minds and their interrelationship. His insights are often invaluable for those involved in ministries of psychological healing.

25. C. G. Jung, *Memories, Dreams, Reflections*, recorded and edited by Aniela Jaffé (New York: Pantheon Books: A Division of Random House, 1963), p. 187-8.

26. Georgia Harkness, *Mysticism: Its Meaning and Message* (Nashville: Abingdon, 1963), p. 22.

27. From an unpublished letter of C. S. Lewis to Dom Bede Griffiths, O.S.B., undated (ca. July 1936), Wade Collection, Wheaton College.

28. St. Patrick's Breastplate.

29. One of the gifts of the Holy Spirit is that of the Word of Knowledge, and has to do with a way of *knowing* peculiar to the so-called unconscious mind. This mind is the seat of the creative imagination, the memory, and the gifts of the Holy Spirit, the intuitive rather than the reasoning faculty.

30. Lewis, *Perelandra*, p. 61.

31. Ibid.

32. John 14:8-26, 31; Luke 4:1, 4:14, 5:17; Acts 1:2; Eph. 3:11-3.

33. This is the supernaturalism that makes up Lewis's mysticism.

34. Lewis, *Weight of Glory*, pp. 16-29.

35. Lewis, *Miracles*, p. 115.

Appendix: The Great Divorce

1. Lewis, *Great Divorce*, p. 5.

2. Eph. 6:12, NEB.

3. Mark 3:28-9.

4. Lewis, *Mere Christianity*, p. 45, note.

5. Lewis, *Screwtape*, second Preface.

6. A phrase Charles Williams quotes and uses. See Williams's *Witchcraft: A History of Black Magic in Christian Times* (New York: World Publishing Co., 1971), pp. 70-5.

7. Jung, *Memories, Dreams, Reflections*, p. 92.

8. Ibid., p. 13.

9. Phallicism or phallism: worship of the generative power in nature, symbolized by phallic art, as in the Dionysian festivals of ancient Greece.

10. Jung, *Memories, Dreams, Reflections*, p. 150.

11. Ibid.

12. Ibid., pp. 152-3.

13. Ibid., p. 168.

14. The novels of D. H. Lawrence are an excellent case in point.

15. Jung, *Memories, Dreams, Reflections*, p. 209.

16. Ibid., p. 255.

17. Ibid., p. 256.

18. Lewis expresses his wonder at the gift of consciousness but interprets the gift differently. In the following lines he views this great gift from the perspective of nature and the body: "And but for our body one whole realm of God's glory—all that we receive through the senses—would go unpraised." *Letters to Malcolm*, p. 17.

19. Lewis, *Letters of Lewis*, p. 196.

20. I know that this book on Lewis would never have been written had I not first read Charles Williams and been overwhelmed with what H. V. D. Dyson called "clotted glory from Charles," Lewis, *Letters of Lewis*, p. 197. Williams's imagery, his "clotted glory," produced such a riot of reactions and ideas in me that I could not but interact with both them and him. I think he had this same effect on Lewis and on Dorothy Sayers; and I have witnessed this same effect on scores of the keenest students. We all owe him a great deal.

21. Williams, *Descent of Dove*, p. 212.

22. Charles Williams, *The English Poetic Mind* (New York: Russell and Russell, 1963), p. 15.

23. Williams interpreted Dante's *Inferno* as differing states of man in himself and the *Purgatorio* as states of the purifying of the images of selfish man. See *Poetry at Present* and *The English Poetic Mind*, both by Charles Williams.

24. The character of Wentworth in Williams's *Descent Into Hell* is an incredible artistic revelation of an unchanging image that bears no more becoming and therefore descends into the hell of self. Many persons, students mostly, who after reading *Descent Into Hell*, cry out that they are such a one. Their lives change after such a revelation.

25. Charles Williams, "The Right of the Passion," in *Three Plays* (London: Oxford University Press, 1931), p. 190.

26. Charles Williams, *Collected Plays* (London: Oxford University Press, 1963), p. vii.

27. Obviously Milton does not recognize an ultimate dualism. In his epic, Satan is the opposite not of God, but of the archangel Michael. Milton's view of evil is Augustinian.

28. Alice Mary Hadfield, *An Introduction to Charles Williams* (London: Robert Hale, 1959), p. 127.

29. Ibid., p. 170.

30. Charles Williams, *Charles Williams Selected Writings,* selected by Anne Ridler (London: Oxford University Press, 1961), pp. 99-100.

31. Glen Cavaliero, "Diagram of Glory" (Ph.D. diss., St. Catherine's College, Cambridge University, n.d.), p. 141.

32. Lewis, *Screwtape,* p. vii.

33. Mark 3:28.

34. Lewis, *Problem of Pain,* p. 72.

35. Lewis, *Mere Christianity,* p. 152.

36. Ibid.

37. Ibid., p. 153.

38. Thomas Binney, hymn, "Eternal Light," ca. 1826, in *The Hymnal of the Protestant Episcopal Church in The United States of America* (New York: Church Pension Fund, 1940), no. 478.

39. Mr. Alexander Solzhenitsyn is the other great twentieth-century prophet crying out to an age that has reconciled good and evil and therefore cannot apply moral criteria to any situation, political or personal. The understanding that between good and evil there is an unbridgeable gap is key in his thought even as it is in Lewis's.

40. Lewis, *Till We Have Faces,* pp. 290-1.

41. Lewis, *Pilgrim's Regress,* p. 177.